TWENTY-FIVE SHORT PLAYS

Twenty-Five Short Plays

Selected Works from the University of North Carolina Long Story Shorts Festival, 2011–2015

Edited by Dana Coen

The Writing for the Screen and Stage Program |
THE UNIVERSITY OF NORTH CAROLINA AT CHAPEL HILL

© 2017 by Dana Coen. All rights reserved.

The plays in this volume are fully protected under the copyright laws of the United States of America. Individual playwrights have retained copyright to their own works. Permission to reproduce these plays, wholly or in part, by any method, must be obtained from the copyright owners or their agents. The playwrights' email addresses are on the title page of each work.

Published by the University of North Carolina at Chapel Hill's Writing for the Screen and Stage Program, 204 Swain Hall, CB 3285, Chapel Hill, NC 27599-3285, rcoen@unc.edu

Distributed by the University of North Carolina Press
www.uncpress.org

ISBN 978-1-4696-3575-0 (pbk.)
ISBN 978-1-4696-3576-7 (ebook)

Front cover image by Laura Azar taken from promotional posters for the Long Story Shorts One Act Festival.
Copyright © Laura Azar.

This volume of plays is dedicated to the late Michael Piller and his wife, Sandra. Without their generous support the Writing for the Screen and Stage Program, the Long Story Shorts Festival, and this publication would not be possible.

Contents

xi Foreword ix

xv About the Writing for the Screen and Stage Program

PLAYS (alphabetized by author)

1 Interred with Their Bones | ALEXANDRIA AGBAJE
A father visits a therapist in purgatory.

11 Chill Pill (Or the Pedantic Pandemic of America) |
ROBERT BAKER
Politically correct reunites with socially correct.

21 Bad Company | WILLIAM G. BOOTH
In the aftermath of the 1929 crash, an investment firm gives up its darkest secret.

29 When the Bell Rings You Shut the **** Up | JIM BULLUCK
A feuding couple becomes a therapist's nightmare.

41 Crisco | ARIEL BUTTERS
A teenager returns home from the hospital after an attempted suicide.

51 Out of the Woods | KRISTEN CHAVEZ
An investigator refuses to give up on the disappearance of a local teenager.

63 Pegging Out | BRONWEN CLARK
Two brothers trapped in a British coal mine consider their destinies.

75 The Split | BRYANT CLEMENTS
After a bad breakup, a young man finds himself caught between the opposing views of his roommates.

87   Hold Onto Me | JESSICA FILLHABER
     A traumatized middle-aged couple struggles to find the way back to each other.

95   Knives Make It Personal | HANNAH FLOYD
     A stage director tries to manipulate an actor into playing against type.

105 The Way Out | COLE HAMMACK
     Two unrelated women are linked by tragedy.

117 Seasoning | XINGYUE SARAH HE
     A newly arrived foreign couple offers assistance to a troubled neighbor.

127 A Failuretale | ELIZABETH HYLTON
     Three Disney princesses confront relationship issues.

139 Snowmen | CHARLIE KELSEY
     A Christmas reunion reveals unfinished business between two brothers.

149 Against the Clock | JACK LIVINGSTON
     An ex–football pro visits his former teammate.

159 Death and Dignity | SCHYLER HOPE MARTIN
     A coroner performs his most personal autopsy.

167 Shot through the Heart | JENNIFER MORGAN
     A young television actress attempts to navigate her feelings toward her co-star.

181 The Rabbit | BROOKE ODOM
     A British mystery writer narrates her own crime story.

193 Amendment | RYAN PASSER
     A congressman and two constituents struggle to resolve the tragic event that has brought them together.

205 The Sixth Chamber | ADAM ROPER
     A man who plays superheroes at children's parties attempts to rescue his wife from a rival.

217 Bad Connection | RACHEL SCHMITT
     Device-addicted college students struggle to communicate.

229 Vinegar Syndrome | RACHEL SHOPE
     A woman's marriage is challenged by the characters in the film she's restoring.

241 Foul | LADARIAN SMITH
     A college basketball player narrates the story of his relationship with a rival/lover.

249 Inside Out | LAURA STOLTZ
     A pregnant woman struggles to reveal her self-destructive impulses.

259 Jumpers and Anchors | LAUREN WINN
     A young man, perched on the girder of a bridge, is interrupted by an intruder with a camera.

267 Acknowledgments

269 Editor's Biography

Foreword

In 2010, as I was reading the first set of short plays by a UNC Writing for the Screen and Stage class, I was struck by the ambition, depth of vision, and singular voices of these undergraduates. The experience encouraged me to imagine a play festival where student writers could participate in a process rarely experienced on their level: a collaborative, developmental environment led by accomplished faculty and working professionals. This was the birth of the Writing for the Screen and Stage Long Story Shorts One Act Festival, in which I select a group of short plays from the program's introductory class and lead the playwrights through a succession of drafts prior to the first day of rehearsal. The plays are then further polished by the ideas of the directors and actors and, in some instances, by the unexpected demands of reality.

The festival premiered in the fall of 2011 on a flexible set that spells out WSS, the program's initials. The first two years of the festival featured full productions of six plays. In 2013, I changed the format to eight plays performed as staged readings. This reduced the rehearsal and production demands, while increasing the number of plays that could be showcased. The intention, in either form, has been to create an experience that mirrors the demands of the professional world, thus preparing students to better handle its challenges.

The plays in this volume were selected from the festival's first five years: 2011 to 2015. As of this writing, forty-four have been presented to audiences at the Kenan and Studio 6 theatres on the UNC campus. I do not stipulate style or impose constraints. Some are one-scene, one-set plays. But others are defined by theatrical devices or have multiple scenes, allowing them to be staged in a variety of ways. What I find encouraging is that nearly all of them were written by first-time playwrights. It is my expectation that, as these young writers continue to develop their craft and collaborative skills, they will honor the Writing for the Screen and Stage Program and the University of North Carolina with their success.

Dana Coen
Director, UNC Writing for the Screen and Stage Program

Long Story Shorts dress rehearsal, October 2015. Set design by Rob Hamilton. Set construction by Ray Dickie.

About the Writing for the Screen and Stage Program

In 1998, television writer/producer Michael Piller, whose many credits include co-creator of the series Star Trek: Voyager and Deep Space Nine, pledged a generous sum to establish a nationally distinctive screenwriting program at his alma mater, the University of North Carolina at Chapel Hill.

In 2003, with the support of these funds, former television and motion picture writer, producer, and executive David Sontag and UNC Senior Associate Dean for Arts and Humanities Darryl Gless launched Writing for the Screen and Stage, an undergraduate minor in dramatic writing. The program, housed and nurtured in the UNC Department of Communication, is designed as an interdisciplinary course of study that taps into the university's historic strengths in dramatic art, communication studies, and the English department's creative writing program. Mr. Sontag retired in 2011 and was replaced by produced playwright and former television writer/producer Dana Coen.

Writing for the Screen and Stage employs a holistic approach in teaching both screenwriting and playwriting disciplines. Traditionally, they are taught separately. But popular theatre, film, and television storytelling all emerged from the same Western dramatic tradition. The minor was designed to recognize their common roots and offer students an integrated writing curriculum that allows for a more immersive and complete understanding of the form, one that enriches and enhances their ability to tell meaningful and compelling dramatic stories in all mediums. Freshman and sophomore students from all corners of the UNC universe are invited to apply during the winter/spring semester. Selection is competitive, with as many as eighteen applicants accepted on an annual basis.

The minor's intensive, two-year curriculum emphasizes the craft of dramatic writing as well as its social, political, and cultural impact. Required courses are Introduction to Writing for the Screen and Stage, Play Analysis, History of American Screenwriting, Intermediate Screenwriting, and Master Screenwriting. Recommended electives include Introduction to Writing for Film and Television, Writing the One-Hour TV Drama, Introduction to Screen Adaptation, Film Story Analysis, and Visual Storytelling. Over the course of their two years in the program, students are required to write a short play, a short screenplay, and a feature-length screenplay.

Graduates of the program are currently enjoying careers in theatre, television, and film, including the production of Off Broadway plays, staff positions and episode assignments on television series, the production of dramatic Internet content, and executive positions in media companies and literary agencies.

Interred with Their Bones

BY ALEXANDRIA AGBAJE

Copyright © by Alexandria Agbaje. All rights reserved. Published with permission from the author. Inquiries concerning rights should be addressed to Alexandria Agbaje at alexandria.agbaje@gmail.com.

Interred with Their Bones

Presented October 3, 2014 | Swain Hall, Studio 6 Theatre, UNC Department of Communication | Directed by Joseph Megel

CHARACTERS

Original cast members are in brackets.

AMI 20s, female, therapist [Angela Santucci].

LELAND PALMER 50s, male [Michael Shannon].

TIME & SETTING

Present. Limbo.

LIGHTS UP

On a therapist's office where AMI PACES in front of a desk. She's giving herself a pep talk.

AMI Be tough. Take him down, right in the throat. You are so close.

[*She sits and sighs determinedly, trying to compose herself. She puts on an indifferent expression then RINGS a bell on her desk. There is a KNOCK KNOCK KNOCK at her door. LELAND PALMER ENTERS.*]

LELAND Yes, Hi. I'm here to see an angel about getting into heaven.

AMI Mr. Palmer, I've been expecting you. Have a seat.

LELAND Please, call me Leland. [*reading her name plate*] Dr. Ami, the Angel of Truth. Licensed Senior Therapist. Senior? What does that mean?

AMI It means I'm the best you've got.

LELAND Oh. Okay. Do you have to go to school for this in heaven, or were you a therapist before you died?

AMI [*ignoring the question*] So, you're having trouble with your memory, right?

LELAND Uh, yes. And they say I can't ascend without knowing my. . . .

AMI . . . . cause of death. Yes. How long do you think you've been in limbo?

LELAND I don't know. Two weeks, maybe?

AMI I see. Why don't we just begin, then? We'll start with a series of questions. Okay?

LELAND Okay. Yeah, I'm an open book. Ask me anything. Name's Leland Palmer, born February seventh in Seattle, height, five foot eight. I am. . . . well, was, a real estate agent, all-around family man.

AMI Age when died?

LELAND Uh. . . . sixty-eight?

AMI No. You were forty-seven.

LELAND Wow, earlier than expected.

AMI Place of death?

LELAND Uhhh. . . . On a toilet. . . . while eating a sandwich?

AMI Your hometown, in a real estate office. Please take this seriously.

LELAND [*feigning remembering*] Oh, yeah. Go Hawks!

AMI Mom and Dad, what were they like?

LELAND [*excited*] I remember! My Mom died young. My Dad was strict.

AMI   A devout Catholic.

LELAND   Oh yes. Kept a cross in every room. Wait, if you have all of this information, why don't you just tell me. . . .

AMI   . . . . how you died? It's either therapy, or staying here forever.

LELAND   Forever? But I need to get to heaven to see my daughter. You see, we ended on such a bad note. I just want to tell her I love her. Can't you understand that?

[*Ami's expression melts for a brief moment. She gives Leland a sympathetic then agitated look, rubs her neck.*]

AMI   I do. I had a father very much like you.

[*Leland tries to comfort her by patting her on the knee, but she recoils.*]

AMI   Let's try a more unconventional method. I'm going to hypnotize you.

[*She pulls out a watch on a long chain, places it in front of his face, and starts moving it back and forth.*]

LELAND   Oh. I tried it once at an office party it didn't. . . . it didn't. . . .

[*He succumbs, closes his eyes.*]

AMI   Think deeply. You're on a trail in the woods, walking towards a house. Can you see it?

LELAND   Yes.

AMI   Do you recognize the house?

LELAND   My real estate office.

AMI   What do you see through the upstairs window?

LELAND   Not much. It's night. Wait, there's a light. A silhouette.

AMI   Who's there?

LELAND   I don't know. My wife? It looks like my wife.

AMI Are you sure? Call her name.

LELAND Catherine! Catherine!

AMI Can she hear you?

LELAND She looks through the window. She sees me. I wave, but she's not waving back. The lights turn off.

AMI Go check it out.

LELAND I'm trying to. I stumble up the porch stairs. I'm angry.

AMI Are you at the door yet?

LELAND Yes.

AMI Open it.

LELAND I don't want to.

AMI Don't you want to see your wife?

LELAND It's not my wife.

AMI Who is it?

LELAND I open the door. I go down the hallway to my main office. The safe is wide open. All the money is gone. A thief!

AMI What's that noise?

LELAND It's coming from the bathroom. I sprint. I'm drunk. I keep falling.

AMI Who's in the bathroom?

LELAND I don't know! I can't see. I'm so angry. I find the light switch. [*gasps*] There's a body on the floor!

[*Ami puts on a large, baggy coat, a thick pair of black glasses, and ties her hair in a ponytail on the side of her head.*]

AMI Go to the body.

LELAND I don't want to.

AMI What if she's hurt?

LELAND I can't.

AMI Do it.

LELAND There are bruises on her neck. She's not breathing. [*beat*] I know who it is.... my daughter.

AMI Call out to her.

LELAND Laura! [*aghast*] She's been strangled.

AMI And the money?

LELAND In her coat pockets.

AMI Who strangled her?

LELAND [*to Laura*] I told you this would happen if you kept it up!

AMI Who strangled her, Mr. Palmer. Leland? Leland. [*in a higher-pitched voice*] Daddy!

[*Leland's eyes quickly open.*]

LELAND Laura? What are you doing in my office so late at night?

AMI [*as LAURA*] I, uh, just left some of my homework here, is all.

LELAND This doesn't look like homework to me!

[*Leland pushes his hand into one of Ami's coat pockets and pulls out wads of cash.*]

LELAND What should I do with you? I've tried everything!

[*Ami, as LAURA, tries to lunge past Leland and escape, but he intercepts and strikes her cheek. She recoils in surprise.*]

AMI [*as LAURA*] Daddy, you're drunk. Why don't we both just go to bed and talk about this in the morning?

LELAND First the drugs, now this? I wish Jessica were my daughter.

AMI [as *LAURA*] What, so you can check out her butt while eating breakfast, too?

LELAND How dare you! You know, most fathers wouldn't go as far as I have to save a soul like yours. Everybody at church says I should kick you out.

AMI [as *LAURA*] Well, I'll save you the trouble. I'm moving in with Bobby!

LELAND Like hell you will!

[*Leland wraps his hands around her neck, and starts STRANGLING her. Ami pretends to struggle, but actually encourages him by grabbing his hands and pushing them tighter around her throat.*]

AMI [as *LAURA*] Is that the best you've got, Dad? Really give it to me!

[*Leland stops and pulls away.*]

LELAND No, I don't want to!

AMI [as *LAURA*] Come on. Do it!

[*Ami, as LAURA, places Leland's hands back around her neck. As she talks, Leland begins to get worked up again, tightening his grip and clenching his teeth.*]

AMI [as *LAURA*] Remember all the times I worried you because I ran away? And when I tried to convince Mom to divorce you?

LELAND Enough!

AMI [as *LAURA*] Oh, and don't forget when I humiliated you in front of Grandpa by wearing that short skirt. He was so disappointed in y. . . .

[*Leland increases his grip. Ami chokes, can no longer speak.*]

LELAND I gave you everything God couldn't. All I asked for was your faith.

[*Leland watches as she loses more air. His expression gradually changes from anger to sadness. As she is just about to pass out, his hands fall from her throat.*]

LELAND I can't. I'm so sorry, Laura. Please forgive me.

AMI [*as LAURA*] Come on!

LELAND I WON'T!

[*She PUSHES him.*]

AMI [*as LAURA*] Why now? Why couldn't you stop then, too? Huh? [*As HERSELF*] Or when you left me on the side of the highway at three a.m.?

LELAND No, I never. . . .

[*She PUSHES Leland harder. He STUMBLES into the chair. He buries his hand in his face as Ami begins THROWING her sweater, glasses, and other objects around her at him.*]

AMI Or when you made Chris and I strangle that cat we wanted to keep as a pet?

LELAND [*confused*] Who's Chris?

AMI And when I caught you cheating on Mom and you locked me in the basement to make me shut up?

LELAND That wasn't me! I never did that.

[*Ami stops, panting. There is a long pause. She looks around the office, then at Leland, realizing where she is.*]

AMI [*calmly*] You're right. It wasn't you. [*beat*] You okay?

[*Leland doesn't respond. He has shut down.*]

AMI   Leland? Leland. Come on. Don't go out on me, now. Please.

[*Ami SHAKES Leland and SNAPS HER FINGERS several times. By the third time, he regains awareness and looks up at her.*]

LELAND   Oh. . . . uh, yes?

AMI   [*weary*] You're done for today. Be sure to check back with my assistant at the front desk.

[*Leland looks around the room, confused.*]

LELAND   Oh, all right. It's over already? Am I any closer?

AMI   We're getting there.

[*Leland makes his way to the door, but turns back to Ami.*]

LELAND   Can I ask you a question? When I get to heaven, is my daughter really going to be there?

AMI   "The evil that men do lives after them; the good is oft interred with their bones."

[*The two let the words silently hang in the air for a still moment.*]

LELAND   Shakespeare.

[*Leland exits. Ami, exasperated, huffs. She returns to her desk, picks up a tape recorder and turns it on. As she talks, she takes out a jar of cream from her desk and rubs it on her neck.*]

AMI   Attempt forty-one thousand, three hundred and forty-eight with patient Leland Palmer. Client has yet to relive his sin. Status remains indefinite. Unable to send him down. Recommended techniques for next session. . . . to be determined.

[*Ami puts down the recorder, but is suddenly overcome. She lets out TWO HEAVY SOBS, slowly recovers, and then begins straightening her hair, clothes, etc. Like before, she RINGS the bell on her desk. There's a KNOCK KNOCK KNOCK at her door. Leland ENTERS.*]

LELAND Hi. . . . Dr. Ami, is it? I'm here to see an angel about getting into heaven.

[*Ami sits back in her chair and sighs.*]

FADE TO BLACK

END OF PLAY

Chill Pill

(Or the Pedantic Pandemic of America)

BY ROBERT BAKER

Copyright © by Robert Baker. All rights reserved. Published with permission from the author. Inquiries concerning rights should be addressed to Robert Baker at rebakeriii@gmail.com.

Chill Pill

(Or the Pedantic Pandemic of America)

Presented October 23, 2015 | Kenan Theatre, UNC Department of Dramatic Art | Directed by Talya Klein

CHARACTERS
Original cast members are in brackets.

JIM 20, male, African American. A world traveler and volunteer [Jerome Allen].

MARTIN LUTHER KING JR. STEVENS 19, male, white. A high school friend of Jim's [Byron Frazelle].

HILLARY CLINTON SHAFFINOWSKI-WILLIAMS 20, female. A barista [Claire Koenig].

TIME & SETTING
Present. A college-town coffee shop.

LIGHTS UP

On a local coffee shop, the Decent Human Bean. JIM, dressed in a dashiki and jeans, sits alone at a small table, waits. ENTER MARTIN LUTHER KING JR. STEVENS. Martin is wearing the same style dashiki as Jim, along with a scarf.

JIM Martin!

MARTIN Jim! Hey, what's up man! Sorry I'm late!

JIM Hey, don't worry about it, dude.

[*The two embrace excitedly.*]

MARTIN Nice shirt. Did you get yours at Suburban Outlier?

JIM It's actually from Uganda.

MARTIN From the village you volunteered at, right? I bought this shirt to raise awareness about their civil war.

JIM [*puzzled*] Uh huh.

MARTIN I'm happy to see we're both doing all we can to help.

JIM That's why I wanted to meet with you, Martin. I was wondering if you'd be interested in helping me build a playground so inner-city kids have a safe place to play.

MARTIN That's a great idea! I'd love to get involved in any way I can! I could post on Facebook that you're looking for volunteers.

JIM I was hoping you'd want to help me build it.

MARTIN That's what the post would be for.

[*Beat. Jim drops it for now. He is still happy to see his friend.*]

JIM I can't believe we haven't seen each other since freshman year.

MARTIN [*correcting him*] First-year year.

[*Jim is confused by this term.*]

MARTIN You meant to say first year. It's more gender inclusive.

JIM Well, okay. That seems fair. First-year year. I'm sure you partied a lot. Did you rush?

MARTIN Oh, that stuff's not really for me. I don't buy into the whole "pay for your friends and become an alcoholic" kind of scene.

JIM That's a little harsh, don't you think?

MARTIN And I saw in a Huffington Post report that one chapter sang a racist chant. Fraternities are all pretty much the same. Might as well all change their names to Kappa Kappa Kappa.

[*This is not the Martin Jim remembers.*]

JIM I don't know if it's fair to generalize like that.

MARTIN I would never try to generalize. It's always important to stay open-minded.

JIM [*playful*] That's good, because I definitely disagree with you on frats.

MARTIN Well, that's fine. But you're wrong.

[*This sets Jim back.*]

MARTIN [*momentarily contrite*] Sorry if I came off kind of stern there. Just a little "healthy debating."

[*Martin begins to take off his scarf.*]

MARTIN Man, it's hot in here. Want to grab an iced coffee?

JIM You go ahead, I shouldn't. I'm giving blood later today.

MARTIN [*nonchalant*] I recently tweeted that people should donate. Guess it worked.

JIM You want to come with me?

MARTIN Oh no, I can't. I have to write my "Social Justice Warriors" blog by six. Tonight's topic is "All White People Are Responsible for What Their Ancestors Did" hashtag, WhiteAintRight, hashtag, WhiteIsntInTheRainbowForAReason. [*beat*] The whites are a terrible people.

JIM *You're* white.

MARTIN Oh, I'm aware, Jim. Trust me. I'm ashamed of it.

JIM You should be proud of who you are, man.

MARTIN There's no such thing as a proud white man; that would be racist. It's the whole reason I changed my name in the first place.

JIM You changed your name?

MARTIN [*proudly*] From Martin Bradley Stevens to Martin Luther King Jr.....Stevens.

JIM [*with disbelief*] Legally?

MARTIN On Facebook.

JIM [*momentarily stunned*] Weren't you going to get coffee?

MARTIN Right.

[*Martin approaches the counter. HILLARY CLINTON SHAFFINOWSKI-WILLIAMS STEPS UP. She wears a traditional barista uniform with a hat and apron that covers the design on her shirt.*]

HILLARY [*cheerfully*] Welcome to the Decent Human Bean! How may I help you?

[*Martin stares at the chalkboard of menu items.*]

MARTIN [*reading as he speaks*] Can I have a "Grounds for an Argument," please? Iced.

HILLARY [*teasing*] Sure thing, hopefully I'll have it to you in shorter time than it takes to get a woman in the Oval Office!

[*Martin and Hillary laugh.*]

HILLARY But no, that would take way too long in our society.

[*Martin glances at Hillary's nametag.*]

MARTIN So, Hillary. Hillary....

HILLARY Clinton.

[*Jim perks up.*]

MARTIN Huh?

HILLARY My name. It's Hillary Clinton. . . . Shaffinowski-Williams.

JIM Hey, look at that! She changed her name like you, Martin!

HILLARY I would never change my name. This is what my birth parents named me.

JIM "Birth" parents? Are you adopted?

HILLARY No. But since they are the parents who gave birth to me, that is what I technically should refer to them as.

[*Martin scoffs.*]

MARTIN [*sarcastic*] Nice pants.

HILLARY [*confused*] Thank. . . . you?

MARTIN What are they, straight fit? GAY fit not good enough for you? Too progressive?

JIM [*concerned*] Martin, what the heck?

HILLARY Actually, these are the pants I'm required to wear.

[*Hillary takes off her apron to reveal a shirt with the diagram of a uterus and ovaries printed on it.*]

HILLARY But I wore this shirt in case anyone forgot what true power looks like.

MARTIN If you wanted to see true power, you would have come watch me tear down that racist "Macy's Red Dot Sale" poster.

JIM Is that why you were late?

MARTIN I will not stand for this racial hatred!

JIM I thought your family was Catholic.

MARTIN I took a BuzzFeed quiz. Told me I was Hindu.

JIM [*not amused*] Martin. . . . please.

HILLARY Well, I wrote an Odyssey article with an open letter to my "future daughter" telling her she could play football or anything else she wanted.

JIM [*earnestly*] I saw a couple of those last week. Which one was yours?

HILLARY I also reassigned every bathroom in the mall to represent a different individual gender identification.

JIM There are like fifty bathrooms in this place; are there even that many gender identities?

HILLARY There are now!

MARTIN [*yelling by the end of the sentence*] Well back at school, I started a petition to end medication for Type Two diabetes because it's just a form of fat shaming!

[*Jim grabs Martin by the arm and begins to pull him aside.*]

JIM Martin! What are you doing?

MARTIN What are you talking about?

JIM Why are you picking a fight with her?

MARTIN She keeps trying to throw all of her petty achievements in my face!

JIM You don't think maybe she's just responding in kind? How about you just be nice to her and stop trying to compete.

MARTIN [*begrudgingly*] Fine. I'll be the bigger person.

[*Martin pulls out his phone, making an exaggerated "check mark" with his finger.*]

MARTIN [*to himself*] Being above her. That's one Gandhi point for me! [*back to Jim*] Be the change you want to see, Jim. Be the change.

[*Martin moves back over to Hillary before Jim has a chance to speak.*]

MARTIN Hey, I think we got off on the wrong foot, I. . . .

HILLARY Forget it. Here's your coffee.

MARTIN This is a pumpkin spice. I ordered an iced coffee.

HILLARY [*baiting*] What, you don't like pumpkin spice?

MARTIN [*defensively*] No, I ordered a "Grounds for an Argument."

HILLARY You've certainly got it! What's wrong with liking pumpkin spice?

MARTIN For starters, there are too many calories, it's too pricey, and I'm really not a fan of the taste.

HILLARY But I bet you love the taste of bacon, huh?

MARTIN [*defensive*] No, I'm not crazy about it. . . . maybe on a salad, but just for the flavor. The texture I can take or leave.

JIM You love bacon.

MARTIN Stay out of this, Jim.

HILLARY A man can love bacon, and it's completely fine. But when a woman wants to express her love for pumpkin spice, it's "annoying"!

MARTIN [*beat*] You're absolutely right.

[*Hillary is stunned. Jim, seeing this as an opportunity to recruit both Martin and Hillary, pulls a folded piece of paper from his pocket.*]

HILLARY So you agree.

MARTIN That any man who likes bacon is a misogynist? Yes. You're right about that.

[*Jim attempts to intervene.*]

JIM If the two of you. . . .

HILLARY It's just like any man who has a dog is actively working toward the exclusion of women.

MARTIN Don't even get me started on that "man's best friend" bullshit!

HILLARY I wish I could find the bigot who came up with that expression and smash his face through a glass ceiling!

[*Jim unfolds the paper.*]

JIM I have this. . . .

HILLARY [*to Martin*] I'm very impressed with your knowledge on women's issues.

MARTIN You have to know your stuff to make the world a better place.

JIM [*raising his voice*] Well, if the two of you are interested in working together to make a difference, I have this volunteer sign-up sheet to help build a playground.

HILLARY I actually could use some help with the troubled kids in my neighborhood.

JIM How are they troubled? Poverty? Hunger?

HILLARY What? No, there's this awful sign hanging up near the playground that reads: "SLOW CHILDREN AT PLAY."

MARTIN You've got to be kidding me!

HILLARY It's extremely insensitive. The sign should clearly say. . . .

MARTIN and HILLARY [*in unison*] "CHILDREN WITH INTELLECTUAL DISABILITIES AT PLAY."

[*FOREIGNER's "Waiting for a Girl Like You" begins to play as Martin and Hillary connect.*]

HILLARY [*smiling*] Exactly.

MARTIN [*to Hillary, flirtatiously*] When you get off, you and I should head back towards your place and. . . . hack that sign down.

HILLARY [*flirting in return*] I like the sound of that. [*excitedly*] Now those kids can safely play in the street without being crushed by words!

JIM Or you could help build the playground. It would be a great gift to these kids.

HILLARY Political correctness is a gift, Jim.

MARTIN Thank you so much for this sign idea, Jim. This is all because of you!

JIM Oh, no. That's okay. Please. Don't mention me if you do this.

HILLARY Let's go right now, Martin. Jim, will you lock up for me?

[*Hillary tosses keys to Jim.*]

MARTIN [*before Jim can answer*] We'll see you at the playground, Jim. Don't forget your bone saw!

JIM No, I don't. . . .

[*Martin and Hillary begin to exit the stage.*]

HILLARY So what's your view on that human-pumpkin, Trump?

[*The LIGHTS begin to SLOWLY FADE.*]

MARTIN Orange better not be the new Black.

[*They LAUGH and EXIT, completely engaged with one another.*]

[*Jim is alone onstage. The line in the song "I've been waiting for a girl like you to come into my life" has been replaced with "I've been waiting for AN INDIVIDUAL OF UNIDENTIFIED GENDER to come into my life." Jim buries his head in his hands.*]

FADE TO BLACK

END OF PLAY

Bad Company

BY WILLIAM G. BOOTH

Copyright © by William G. Booth. All rights reserved. Published with permission from the author. Inquiries concerning rights should be addressed to William G. Booth at WmGBooth@gmail.com.

Bad Company

Presented October 23, 2015 | Kenan Theatre, UNC Department of Dramatic Art | Directed by Talya Klein

CHARACTERS
Original cast members are in brackets.

STUART CROSBY 26, male. An ambitious investment analyst [James Scalise].

GARRETT CUNNINGHAM 52, male. Vice president of an investment firm [John Paul Middlesworth].

SEBASTIAN GREEN 57, male. President of an investment firm [Michael Shannon].

TIME & SETTING
1929. Wall Street investment office.

LIGHTS UP

On an office. Outside the window is a spectacular view of the Brooklyn Bridge. There is a desk with a telephone and a closed briefcase.

GARRETT CUNNINGHAM, dressed in fine business attire, stares out the window.

STUART CROSBY, equally well dressed, but disheveled, ENTERS tentatively with a pile of papers.

CROSBY Mister Cunningham? I've compiled my findings. . . .

[*Cunningham does not respond.*]

CROSBY Sir?

CUNNINGHAM [*continuing to stare out the window*] I hear you, Crosby.

CROSBY I didn't have time to edit, so I apologize if it's a little rough around the edges.

CUNNINGHAM Looks fine to me.

CROSBY Sir, you haven't even seen it.

[*Cunningham, WALKING WITH A NOTICEABLE LIMP, comes around the desk and over to Crosby. He hardly gives the papers a glance.*]

CUNNINGHAM Still looks fine.

CROSBY How about I summarize it for you, Sir?

CUNNINGHAM Good idea.

[*Cunningham returns to his seat.*]

CROSBY Well, we're pinned down right now. . . . and will lose the battle today, but. . . .

GREEN [*offstage*] Everything in order, Garrett?

[*SEBASTIAN GREEN dressed in professional attire, ENTERS.*]

[*Startled, Crosby DROPS his papers, immediately bends down to recover them. Cunningham is unresponsive.*]

GREEN I haven't seen anyone drop to the ground that fast since I was in the Third.

[*Cunningham's detachment tests Green's patience.*]

GREEN Garrett, this isn't the moment to be the strong, silent type, you better open your goddamn mouth.

CROSBY Actually Sir, we were just discussing our. . . . situation.

[*Crosby gives Cunningham a nod. It goes unnoticed. Crosby holds out the papers to Green.*]

CROSBY As you can see, we can have a solid hedge strategy preventing further losses this quarter and then into next.

GREEN I'm sorry, Mister. . . . ?

CROSBY Crosby, Stuart Crosby. We met in your office a couple of weeks ago. I advised we invest in Coca-Cola.

GREEN [*irritated*] Garrett?

[*Cunningham taps the briefcase on the desk and gives a nod. His eyes meet Green's. Relief washes over Green; his demeanor cools.*]

GREEN And how is Coca-Cola faring? A lead balloon like the others, I assume.

CROSBY To be honest, Sir, it's actually doing quite well.

GREEN Well then, good call. Glad to know I have the best and brightest working for me.

CROSBY Thank you, Mr. Green. I'm glad to be on the frontlines alongside you.

GREEN The pleasure is all mine. I better get going. Denise has been holding off investor calls. They want to know how their money grew legs and ran off. Got to hold off the onslaught.

CROSBY How about *I* man the phones, Mr. Green? [*holding up his papers*] I can answer their questions.

GREEN As I understand it, they'd prefer to hear the voice of the president of Green Wealth Management. But I will say, Crosby, if I didn't know better, that could be you someday soon.

CROSBY That's very nice to hear, Sir.

[*Green adjusts Crosby's askew tie.*]

GREEN You even have the look of an executive. Not that looks matter around here. Tell him what matters around here, Garrett.

CUNNINGHAM Results.

[*Green taps the stack of papers.*]

GREEN And that's what you've got right here. I'll have the calls patched through to you.

CROSBY [*flustered*] Now?

GREEN Relax. Take a breather. I can tell you've been up all night. Just stay in here, and you'll be ready when the first call comes in. With the schedule freed, you and I can push up our meeting considerably, Garrett.

[*Cunningham stares back. Green CROSSES toward the office door. He turns back in the doorframe.*]

GREEN Crosby, you'll do just fine.

[*Green EXITS. Cunningham walks to a dry bar and gathers two empty glasses.*]

CROSBY Oh, I don't drink. I like to stay sharp as a tack.

CUNNINGHAM It's about keeping yourself intact. I'd recommend you start or find something else to help you cope.

[*Cunningham sets both glasses down on the desk and motions for Crosby to sit opposite him. Crosby sits.*]

CROSBY All we have to do is make it through today. I don't know what's going to happen at all the other firms, but I'm confident we'll be the ones left standing when the smoke clears.

[*There is a long pause. Crosby flips through his report, brushing up.*]

CUNNINGHAM You ever read the Bible?

[*Cunningham opens the briefcase and withdraws a Bible.*]

CROSBY I appreciate the sentiment, but I think I should probably review my. . . .

[*Cunningham slides the Bible across the table to Crosby. Crosby is bemused.*]

CUNNINGHAM Now would be a great time.

[*Crosby opens the cover. He reaches his hand into the book and removes a canteen that has been hidden inside.*]

CUNNINGHAM French brandy: a parting gift the Army didn't know they gave. It's not cognac, but who can really taste the difference?

[*Crosby, sensing he can't refuse this drink, unscrews the top and takes a sip from the canteen. He COUGHS a bit.*]

CROSBY It's smooth.

[*Crosby hands it back to Cunningham. Cunningham STANDS AND HOBBLES to the window.*]

CROSBY It is quite the view, Sir.

CUNNINGHAM Is it?

CROSBY Yeah, it's amazing. The skyline. The bridge.

CUNNINGHAM I guess I don't see it.

CROSBY You can't see the Brooklyn Bridge?

CUNNINGHAM No, I see a different one. . . . [*long beat*] Our whole squad, thirteen of sixteen men. Dead. It was the staff sergeant, Private O'Reilly, and me stuck. . . . defending the French retreat across that godforsaken bridge. . . . just the three of us left, and more Krauts than sinners in that book.

CROSBY Dear God! I'm so sorry, Sir. I had no idea.

CUNNINGHAM All we had to do was hold position while they pulled back. O'Reilly . . . [*taking a long swig from his canteen*] I've never seen anyone fight so hard. Bullet to the arm. Never stopped shooting. All for that bridge.

CROSBY Did you save it?

CUNNINGHAM No, the staff sergeant stopped feeding me ammunition because....

GREEN [*offstage*] .... we were all doomed.

[*Green ENTERS. He approaches Cunningham, places a hand on his shoulder in eerie solidarity. Cunningham passes him the canteen.*]

GREEN And the corporal agreed, right Garrett? You agreed? So I took the only action I knew would get us out.

[*Green forms a gun with his hand and points it at Cunningham's knee. Cunningham flinches.*]

GREEN I then dragged the corporal out of enemy fire. [*beat*] The story of an American staff sergeant who demonstrated, "Gallantry in action against an enemy of the United States while engaged in military operations involving conflict with an opposing foreign force." At least that's what the Silver Citation Star says.

CROSBY And O'Reilly?

[*Cunningham opens his mouth to speak, but no words come out. There's no justification.*]

CROSBY Sir, what happened to O'Reilly?

GREEN He elected to make the ultimate sacrifice. I gave him a few words of encouragement, and he gave me this. So, I let him fight for God and Country.

CROSBY You left him....

GREEN .... to fight

CROSBY .... to....

CUNNINGHAM .... die. We left him there to die. What does that make us?

[*Silence.*]

CUNNINGHAM Crosby?

CROSBY [*softly*] Cowards.

[*Cunningham gains a sense of peace from hearing this, relaxes slightly.*]

GREEN [*to Cunningham*] Now that you feel better about the past, how about we look to our future?

[*Green polishes off the canteen.*]

GREEN Ready, Garrett?

[*Cunningham stands and picks up the briefcase. Green and Cunningham approach the door of the office.*]

CROSBY What did you say to him?

GREEN Pardon?

CROSBY What did you say to O'Reilly? What were the words of encouragement?

GREEN I said: "O'Reilly, ... you'll do just fine."

[*Green and Cunningham EXIT. Crosby is left stunned. He sips at the cognac as a way to cope.*]

[*Suddenly, TWO GUNSHOTS are heard OFFSTAGE.*]

[*Crosby DASHES TO THE DOOR just as the PHONE on the desk RINGS. He stops midway between the door and the phone. It RINGS again. He's frozen, caught between the two events. ...*]

FADE TO BLACK

END OF PLAY

When the Bell Rings You Shut the **** Up

BY JIM BULLUCK

Copyright © by Jim Bulluck. All rights reserved. Published with permission from the author. Inquiries concerning rights should be addressed to Jim Bulluck at thejimbulluck@gmail.com.

When the Bell Rings You Shut the **** Up

Presented October 25, 2013 | Kenan Theatre, UNC Department of Dramatic Art | Directed by Joseph Megel

CHARACTERS

Original cast members are in brackets.

PATRICIA MARSEILLE 40s, female, upper middle class. A suburban housewife [Elisabeth Lewis Corley].

RONALDO MARSEILLE 40s, male. Patricia's professor husband [John Paul Middlesworth].

DR. DAVID 40s, male. A family therapist [Greg Hohn].

TIME & SETTING

Present. An upscale college town.

LIGHTS UP

On a small therapist's office. PATRICIA MARSEILLE ENTERS and takes a seat on one of the couches. A few moments later, RONALDO MARSEILLE ENTERS carrying a tray with two coffees.

PATRICIA You brought the coffee!

RONALDO [*annoyed*] Yes.

PATRICIA Well, I just figured you would forget.

RONALDO Why do you always assume I forget things?

[*Ronaldo hands Patricia her coffee and sits across from her. She sips it.*]

PATRICIA Is there milk in this?

RONALDO I made sure to get it with milk.

PATRICIA I can't drink milk.

RONALDO What do you mean you can't drink milk?

PATRICIA I'm a vegan, Ron.

RONALDO Well, I know that. I just thought you took your coffee....

PATRICIA Do I need to sit you down for another food documentary?

RONALDO Oh, fuck off. You're such a self-righteous little....

[*Dr. David ENTERS.*]

DR. DAVID Hello, you must....

PATRICIA [*to Ronaldo*] How is it that you forget seemingly everything about me?

RONALDO Because it's all so incredibly fascinating?

DR. DAVID My name is Dr. David, but you can....

PATRICIA [*to Ronaldo*] Well, maybe it's not, but at least in my pathetic little existence I know how my husband takes his coffee.

DR. DAVID You must be the Marseilles. I'm Dr. David. It's nice to meet the both of you.

PATRICIA Oh. Hello. We're here for our four p.m. appointment. You're late.

DR. DAVID Sorry about that.

PATRICIA I don't want an excuse. Anyway, I'm Patricia and this is my husband....

RONALDO Professor Ronaldo Marseille, but please call me Dr. Marseille.

DR. DAVID It seems like you've already gotten started. What seems to be the cause of this tension?

RONALDO Outside of your being late?

PATRICIA My husband here. . . .

RONALDO Oh, for Christ sake!

DR. DAVID Please let her finish, Ron.

RONALDO [*correcting him*] Dr. Marseille.

PATRICIA It seems Ron has the ability to recall exact quotes of dead men from four hundred years ago but not to care about my sacrifices for the animal kingdom.

DR. DAVID Ron, what do you have to say in response to that?

RONALDO It's idiotic.

DR. DAVID And why is that?

RONALDO Well, first off it's quotations, not quotes. Second, why is she upset about a bit of dairy when half her wardrobe consists of furs?

PATRICIA My husband is too dense to see I'm being ironic. Also, I deserve to look nice.

DR. DAVID Okay, okay. Let's stop and take a second. Ron, I'd like you to discuss the problems you've been facing of late.

PATRICIA I still don't think the vegan issue has been. . . .

RONALDO My largest predicament would probably be interacting with the repressed masses. My wife, for instance, won't even engage in a philosophical discussion anymore.

PATRICIA And by that you mean I won't sit around and let you masturbate to your own ego.

DR. DAVID Again, this isn't the place to blame or attack.

RONALDO And you think it's wrong to place blame?

PATRICIA Blame can be necessary.

DR. DAVID I don't think it's. . . .

RONALDO You see, morality is a rudimentary construction based on human perception. No one person should be allowed. . . .

PATRICIA For once, can you stop with your existentialist babble?

RONALDO Good God, Pat, if you are going to belittle, at least be precise in your name-calling. I am an ethical nihilist. My thoughts are not some contrived Sam Beckett bullshit.

PATRICIA You would give Narcissus a run for his money.

RONALDO And you'd give that slut Aphrodite one as well.

DR. DAVID Alright.

[*Dr. David RISES and walks over to his desk. He opens a drawer and pulls out a SHINY CALL BELL.*]

DR. DAVID We are going to practice a lesson in civility. I am going to place this bell on the table. Anytime someone begins to blame or attack, the other will ring the bell. Once the bell is rung, the person speaking must immediately stop or choose to rephrase what they are saying. Is that kosher with both of you?

PATRICIA That's fine by me.

RONALDO Do you think we're Jewish?

DR. DAVID It's just an expression.

RONALDO My name is Dr. Marseille. What kind of idiot would. . . .

[*DING. Dr. David hits the bell.*]

DR. DAVID Thank you, Ron. You provided a perfect example of how the bell will work. Let's get back to the previous topic. Are there any other issues you'd like to address?

RONALDO In addition to the meaninglessness of the universe and the subjugation of human thought?

DR. DAVID Yes, let's say in addition to those.

RONALDO In the University's grand wisdom, they've replaced the coffee machine with some sort of tea station. If my wife would replace the espresso machine she broke....

PATRICIA Well, you have my permission to buy one at any time.

RONALDO Why should I be the one to participate in such activities? After all, it was your....

[*DING. Patricia hits the bell.*]

RONALDO It's true though, I work far too hard....

[*DING. Patricia hits the bell.*]

RONALDO All I was saying is that it would be nice if someone beside myself would help out around the....

[*DING. Patricia hits the bell.*]

DR. DAVID Ron, what I feel like you are trying to say is that marriage is a partnership. You believe you both have specific roles to fill, is that correct?

RONALDO Well, if you want to make me sound like a wanker.

[*DING. Dr. David hits the bell.*]

RONALDO Yes, that is what I mean.

DR. DAVID Well, good. I'm glad we understand each other. Now, Patricia, what's your response to what Ron just said?

PATRICIA I think it's ridiculous.

[*DING. Ronaldo rings the bell.*]

PATRICIA What gives him the right to subjugate me like that? If anything, he should be the homemaker. My salary is far larger....

[*DING. Ronaldo rings the bell.*]

PATRICIA Oh please, stop hitting the bell, you chauvinist.

[*DING. Ronaldo rings the bell.*]

RONALDO This bell bullshit is pretty amusing.

DR. DAVID Ron, please. Patricia, could you express yourself without blaming or attacking your husband?

PATRICIA Considering my job is to defend the persecuted, I believe I do a lot.

RONALDO Getting Wall Street bankers off is. . . .

PATRICIA This in addition to the number of charitable organizations I participate in.

RONALDO You sitting around drinking in the name of the less fortunate is hardly a sacrifice worth fucking bragging. . . .

[*DING. Patricia hits the bell.*]

PATRICIA As opposed to moping about how. . . .

[*DING. Ronaldo hits the bell.*]

PATRICIA You know I find profanity very offensive. For once could you speak with a clean. . . . ?

RONALDO They are just words, God damn it!

[*DING. Patricia hits the bell.*]

RONALDO Shit [*DING*]. Bitch [*DING*]. . . .

DR. DAVID That's enough.

RONALDO Pussy [*DING*]. Cum [*DING*]. Asshole [*DING*]. Fuck [*DING*]. Cunt [*DING*].

DR. DAVID I said that is enough! [*beat*] Okay, how about we discuss something that you both have some common ground with. Do you have children?

RONALDO Ugh.

DR. DAVID Is there a problem?

RONALDO Have they ever been anything but?

PATRICIA Talk about sunk costs.

[*The couple break into LAUGHTER.*]

RONALDO "Take me here. I need a ride to that." They're monsters. Disgusting little monsters.

PATRICIA It's so creepy seeing these putrid miniature versions of yourself running around. Matilda got in quite the hissy fit when I said I was busy during her class recital.

RONALDO Who has the time to sit through two hours of clunky choreography anyway?

PATRICIA It's just plain selfish of her if you think about it.

RONALDO It's like they don't realize how good our lives would be without them.

PATRICIA We gave up our best years. What a waste. Also Sebastian has been spending far too much time alone with that Clements boy.

RONALDO I hope we don't have to raise some fagg....

[*DING. DING. DING. Dr. David hits the bell.*]

DR. DAVID Okay, we are now going to include attacking or blaming anyone in regards to the bell ringing.

RONALDO That seems idiotic.

[*DING. Dr. David hits the bell.*]

PATRICIA So, are we not allowed to discuss our children anymore?

DR. DAVID No, please do, just make sure to not attack or belittle them while you are doing it.

RONALDO I don't see much point in that. [*long beat*] Fuck, what are we allowed to talk about?

DR. DAVID Anything you would like, as long as it doesn't cause the bell to be rung. Can we agree to that?

RONALDO Fine.

PATRICIA All right.

RONALDO We could discuss. . . . no.

PATRICIA What about our terrible neighbor Geor. . . . Sorry.

DR. DAVID That's all right. We can sit here until we a find a productive topic to discuss.

[*Silence.*]

PATRICIA [*to Ronaldo*] How is your friend, um, Mark doing?

RONALDO Max?

PATRICIA Yes, him.

RONALDO The cancer is back.

PATRICIA Oh.

[*Silence.*]

RONALDO All right, I'm tired of this.

DR. DAVID Well. . . .

PATRICIA As am I. I don't think it's effective.

RONALDO [*re: Dr. David*] I wonder where he got his credentials?

PATRICIA I'd put my money on a state school.

DR. DAVID Please, let us focus on the matters at hand.

RONALDO This is a matter I'd like to focus on.

PATRICIA I agree. [*to Dr. David*] Where did you go to school?

DR. DAVID I don't think that's relevant.

PATRICIA Definitely a state school. Probably not even a good one like Berkeley.

RONALDO You know, he reminds me of that awful babysitter.

PATRICIA Oh, Trish? She was the worst. . . . stealing my earrings and then continually lying about it.

RONALDO God, you really gave it to her when you found out.

PATRICIA So melodramatic with the crying.

RONALDO You were so tantalizing as you stood over her, letting her know who was in charge.

PATRICIA Don't give me all the credit. You were quite suave yourself when you told her that we would not be giving her a ride home.

[*The couple share a LAUGH.*]

RONALDO Didn't you find those a few weeks ago?

PATRICIA What?

RONALDO The earrings.

PATRICIA Come to think of it, I did.

[*DING. Dr. David rings the bell.*]

DR. DAVID Let's get back on track.

RONALDO [*To Patricia*] Can you believe all this bell shit he keeps doing?

PATRICIA I know! It's so obnoxious. Is this place a therapist's office or a diner?

DR. DAVID That's enough. We're here to focus on your issues.

RONALDO What if our issues are about you?

[*Patricia LAUGHS.*]

DR. DAVID The session is nearly halfway over. You both stand to benefit. . . .

[*DING. Ronaldo hits the bell.*]

DR. DAVID Please don't ring the bell out of turn. It violates. . . .

[*DING. Patricia hits the bell.*]

DR. DAVID You can play jokes all you want, but you both need serious counseling.

[*DING. Patricia and Ronaldo both ring the bell. They RISE as they speak.*]

RONALDO David. Please don't attack or blame.

PATRICIA Could you rephrase what you were saying?

DR. DAVID Sit down.

[*The couple disobeys. Dr. David suddenly picks up the bell and THROWS IT across the room.*]

DR. DAVID I said sit down!

[*They sit.*]

DR. DAVID Ron! [*beat*] I want you to take a moment for self-examination. You present yourself as an intellectual, but you're not smart enough to be accepted as one. Have you ever considered who could love you? Truly love you? Love such a sad, pathetic man?

PATRICIA This is quite unprof. . . .

DR. DAVID And you. Patricia Marseille. A woman who defends the rich and takes from the poor. You claim to support animal rights, yet you have no real interest in them. You're smarter than your pedantic husband, which makes it all the more depressing because you have some awareness of how repugnant a person you actually are.

RONALDO You have no right to speak to my wife....

DR. DAVID Ron. Pat. I want you to take a second and look at one another. You are miscreations, seemingly unlovable. Neither of you have any redeeming qualities worth noting. Yet! In the great comedy that is the universe, you found each other. You found someone just as horrendous, just as treacherous as yourself. While you may be ugly people both inside and out, think of how beautiful it is you happened upon each other. Take a second and think about that.

[*Silence as they do.*]

DR. DAVID Now, Ron?

RONALDO Yes?

DR. DAVID I want you to take Pat in your arms.

[*He does.... carefully.*]

DR. DAVID And Pat?

PATRICIA Yes?

DR. DAVID I want you to look at your husband and tell him you love him.

PATRICIA [*beat*] I love you.

DR. DAVID Now what do you say, Ron?

RONALDO [*beat*] I love you, too.

DR. DAVID Good. [*long beat*] Now, get the fuck out of my office!

BLACKOUT

END OF PLAY

Crisco

BY ARIEL BUTTERS

Copyright © by Ariel Butters. All rights reserved. Published with permission from the author. Inquiries concerning rights should be addressed to Ariel Butters at ArielLynnButters@gmail.com.

Crisco

Premiered October 6, 2011 | Swain Hall, Studio 6 Theatre, UNC Department of Communication | Directed by Paul Ferguson

CHARACTERS

Original cast members are in brackets.

EVELYN LARDER 15, female. Just released from a psychiatric hospital [Melanie Johnson].

DIANE LARDER 40s, female. Evelyn's mother [Jennifer Stander].

BOB LARDER 40s, male. Evelyn's father [Estes Tarver].

CARTER LARDER 21, male. Evelyn's brother [Scott Vicari].

WAITER 30s, male [Colin Warren Hicks].

HOMELESS MAN 50s, male [Korde Tuttle].

CRISCO The homeless man's small dog [Phoebe].

TIME & SETTING

Present. Inside a car, suburban dining room, inside and outside a restaurant.

SCENE ONE

LIGHTS UP

On the two front seats of a CAR. DIANE LARDER is driving with her daughter, EVELYN. Diane is upbeat, but Evelyn is sullen, stares ahead.

DIANE Daddy totally reseeded the lawn, y'know. You won't even recognize the yard.

[*Diane looks at her daughter and smiles, waiting for a response that she does not get.*]

DIANE Carter's so excited you're coming home. It's crazy to think he hasn't seen you since he left at the beginning of the semester. He thinks about you all the time, though.

[*Diane pats Evelyn's leg. She stares ahead, motionless.*]

DIANE [*excitedly*] Oh! And, we got you a new bed. . . . on a whim this morning, at the mall with Carter. Dr. Jonas says that sleeping soundly is the first step to success, so we picked out the most successful-looking one we could find.

[*Beat. Diane strokes her daughter's hair and smiles. Evelyn says nothing.*]

END OF SCENE

SCENE TWO

BOB, Evelyn's father, sits at the dining table. Diane and Evelyn ENTER.

DIANE We're home! Carter, we're home! Beautiful day out, perfect day for our baby to come home.

BOB [*to Evelyn*] Sure is. Hey, kiddo, how's it going?

[*Evelyn sits down next to him at the table. She reaches for a stray section of the paper.*]

DIANE Evelyn, we have dinner reservations at Margaux's tonight. It only seems fit that we celebrate your recovery at your favorite restaurant.

BOB [*without looking up*] They've got great sole piccata.

DIANE They do, they most certainly do. [*yelling off*] Carter, your sister's home! Come see your sister! Evelyn, I swear your friends have just been calling off the hook. I made a list of everyone, the date they called, their numbers, and if they asked anything specific. I taped it right here by the phone. They've missed you so much! Can I get you anything, baby? A soda? Toast?

[*Evelyn looks up from her paper. She RISES and prepares herself a glass of water. While she's pouring from the pitcher, her brother, CARTER, BOUNDS IN.*]

CARTER Evelyn! What's up, little sis?

[*He picks her up off the ground into a bear hug, spilling her water. She frowns and glares at him. He ruffles her hair. She shrinks away from his touch.*]

CARTER [*offended*] What, you're not talking to me?

DIANE Carter! Don't be rude to your sister. She doesn't have to talk if she doesn't want to.

[*Carter throws up his hands in confusion. Evelyn returns to her newspaper.*]

DIANE [*to Carter*] Help me bring in Evelyn's new bed from the garage?

[*Diane EXITS in a hurry. Carter glares disapprovingly at his unresponsive sister as he answers.*]

CARTER Sure, Mom.

[*He EXITS stage right. Immediately after he EXITS, Bob SIGHS.*]

BOB [*reading the newspaper pensively*] Let's see what Betty and Veronica are up to this week.

[*Evelyn lowers her paper to look at her father. She is silent but attentive.*]

BOB [*reading as he goes*] Betty says, "Veronica, what color is your prom dress?" Veronica says, "I'm not telling you, Betty," and Betty says, "But if we have the same color prom dress, I'll just have to...."

[*Bob cuts the final words off and clears his throat, quickly changing the subject. Evelyn stares at him.*]

BOB [*rambling uncomfortably*] Never mind, I think I read that one last week. The comics these days, they're really lacking. I heard there might even be a comic strike. You know what, I bet that's why they reprinted this one. They didn't have any new material because the artists are on strike.

[*Sensing her father's discomfort, Evelyn reaches a hand across the table to cover his. He looks up at her.*]

BOB I'm sorry, baby. It was distasteful, that's why I stopped reading it. Nothing funny about it. They'd think differently about the situation if they'd been through the roller coaster we have.

DIANE [*offstage*] EVELYN!

[*Diane ENTERS*]

DIANE Evelyn, could you help your brother with this behemoth of a bed? I really don't think I'm spry enough, and you know your father has a bad back. I'm sorry to make you lug your own gift, but I don't see how else we're going to get it in the house. Bob, could you help bring in all the bedding and extra pieces from the car? I still haven't unloaded them and it will be at least a few trips.

[*Bob, Evelyn, and Diane all EXIT. Carter is heard SHOUTING.*]

CARTER [*offstage*] Okay, move right. Wait, no, my right. Your left. Okay. Do you have a good grip?

[*Carter and Evelyn slowly ENTER, haphazardly carrying a massive bed, mattress, and frame together. Carter leads by walking backward. Evelyn ENTERS a few paces behind.*]

CARTER [*getting angry*] Could you at least, like, nod your head or something? I'm trying to communicate here. I'm dropping this side. Pick it up.

[*Evelyn is clearly struggling to hold up the bed. She grimaces and glares at her brother.*]

CARTER [*raising his voice*] No, the other side, Evie! Do you have it or not? God, just grunt or something!

[*Evelyn fumbles for the correct side and ends up dropping the bed on Carter's foot. He CRIES OUT in pain. She EXITS in a hurry. Diane ENTERS.*]

DIANE [*peppy*] How's it going, guys? It's a big thing, huh? So pretty, though, with the headboard, and it looks really.... [*realizing things have gone awry*] Where's Evelyn?

CARTER She dropped the bed on me and ran away! Geez, I think she could have broken my toe.

DIANE She obviously didn't mean to drop the bed.

CARTER You know what, Mom, I don't know what she means because she's not using any *words*!

DIANE [*shaking head*] Dr. Jonas said she'd start talking as soon as she got in a comfortable....

[*Carter gestures for Diane to be quiet as Evelyn ENTERS, carrying a plastic bag filled with ice.*]

DIANE [*upbeat*] Oh, Evelyn! How nice of you! Here, Carter, put this on your foot. [*to Evelyn*] Dinner reservations are in an hour, baby. Why don't you go get ready?

[*Evelyn obediently trots off stage.*]

END OF SCENE

SCENE THREE

An upscale restaurant. All four family members are seated at a table.

DIANE Evelyn, you know your brother has been working on a community project in New Haven that focuses on teens battling depression.

CARTER [*grumbling*] Yeah, except they actually talk.

DIANE Carter! This celebration is for your sister, who has had a very difficult year. Now please just can the sass for one night so we can at least pretend to be normal.

[*A WAITER enters, carrying plates of food.*]

WAITER [*to Carter*] Braised chicken with grilled kale. [*to Bob*] Sole piccata.

[*The Waiter takes a deep breath before handing Diane her food.*]

WAITER Sole piccata, minus the sole plus the halibut, with asparagus instead of capers and a lemon-free sauce.

[*He hands Evelyn a plate.*]

WAITER This is what you were pointing to, right?

[*Evelyn smiles and nods. The waiter EXITS politely. Before even looking at her own dish, Diane cranes her neck curiously over the table to see what her daughter has ordered.*]

DIANE [*sweetly*] Filet mignon? Oh, sweetie, you can't eat that. Here, let me get the waiter back, and we'll get you something better.

CARTER Why can't she eat that?

DIANE [*under her breath*] No sharp objects.

CARTER [*laughing heartily*] What, like she's just going to stab herself in the middle of the restaurant? [*realization*] Oh my God, you took away all of our steak knives, didn't you? When did you even do that?

DIANE [*ignoring Carter; to Evelyn*] Sweetie, you're going to have to eat that with a butter knife.

[*Evelyn SUDDENLY RISES and searches the table, finding no knife.*]

DIANE Evelyn, honey, I had them taken away, there's none here on the table.

[*Evelyn indignantly STOMPS OVER to a dining cart.*]

DIANE Evie, now just where are you going? Don't be mad, honey, it's for your own safety.

[*Evelyn pulls a steak knife out of the tray and triumphantly holds it above her head.*]

DIANE Evelyn, what are you doing? That is so rude, Evelyn, please just come back to your. . . .

[*Evelyn returns to the table and points the knife angrily at her mother, who GASPS loudly.*]

DIANE Evelyn! This is so embarrassing.

[*Evelyn calmly returns to her seat and begins cutting up her food.*]

DIANE Honestly, Evelyn, was that really necessary? You could have just asked for a steak knife.

BOB Why would she have asked? It's not like you would have given it to her.

DIANE Well, of course I would have.

BOB What, so depriving her of everyday objects is some sort of punishment for not talking? Like you'll reward her with the object she needs if she just uses words?

CARTER Dude, I totally thought she was just going to stab herself in the middle of the restaurant.

DIANE Bob, would you please stop putting words in my mouth? I am just trying to do what's best for Evelyn.

BOB No, you're not, you're trying to do what it takes to sweep our problems under the rug and pretend like nothing ever happened. And I don't have to put words in your mouth because there are enough of them spilling out all of the time anyway!

DIANE Robert! You know what, this was a terrible idea. We weren't ready for this.

CARTER So, you want to leave or something?

BOB Doubtful. Leaving before eating would cause a scene. As if we haven't already.

DIANE Bob, I am really hurt by the way you're speaking to me right now.

[*Suddenly, Evelyn LAUNCHES FROM HER CHAIR and EXITS. Diane calls after her.*]

DIANE Are you going to the bathroom, sweetie? Okay! Good luck! Be careful! I'll come check on you in a little while!

[*Diane lowers her voice to speak with her son and husband.*]

DIANE Goodness, she's sucked down so many Cokes, I'm not surprised she has to pee this early through the meal. And in such a rush.

[*They return to their meals.*]

END OF SCENE

SCENE FOUR

The street outside the restaurant. Evelyn EXITS to find a HOMELESS MAN SINGING "Always Look on the Bright Side of Life." She lets out an exasperated sigh and then plops down next to him and his small DOG.

HOMELESS MAN Well, hello there. I don't suppose you're here to give me money. Usually people who do just throw it and run. You want a smoke or something? I just finished my last one. You got a smoke or something?

[*Evelyn shakes her head.*]

HOMELESS MAN Not talking, huh? That's okay, you can just sit and keep me company.

[*Evelyn smiles at the man. She is at ease in his presence.*]

HOMELESS MAN You don't talk, but do you sing? I like to sing.

[*He breaks out again into his SONG for a moment. Evelyn leans forward to pat the dog.*]

HOMELESS MAN That's Crisco. I named her that 'cause I found her in an alley licking the inside of a Crisco can. See that wound on her leg? Last week some mangy mutt got a hold of her. Some guy, I guess a vet or something, gave me some gauze and alcohol, but he said the bite looked bad. Do you think it looks bad? Crisco's my best friend. I don't want anything to happen to her, but it's not like I can pay a vet bill. What do you think I should do?

DIANE [*RUSHES OUT, panicked*] EVELYN! EVELYN! Oh my God, EVELYN!

[*Carter and Bob FOLLOW.*]

DIANE [*furious*] EVELYN! What the hell are you doing out here? You told us you were going to the bathroom! No, wait, you didn't tell us, because you're not talking. You know, we're really doing the best we can here, but it would be really fucking nice if you could throw us a bone or something. It's not like I took some special parenting class on emotionally unstable adolescent girls that's supposed to help me handle this. I don't know what to do as much as anyone else does, so. . . .

BOB [*interrupting*] Diane, please, would you just shut up? For once, SHUT UP!

[*A startled Diane shuts down. For the first time, there is LONG, GLORIOUS SILENCE. Evelyn continues to pet Crisco the dog. Then. . . .*]

EVELYN [*to the Homeless Man*] I think all she needs is time to heal.

[*The Homeless Man nods in agreement. The family looks on listening. . . . just listening.*]

FADE TO BLACK

END OF PLAY

Out of the Woods

BY KRISTEN CHAVEZ

Copyright © by Kristen Chavez. All rights reserved. Published with permission from the author. Inquiries concerning rights should be addressed to Kristen Chavez at chavez.km@gmail.com.

Out of the Woods

Premiered November 15, 2012 | Swain Hall, Studio 6 Theatre,
UNC Department of Communication | Directed by Dana Coen

CHARACTERS

Original cast members are in brackets.

MATT HARTNELL 30s, male [Trevor Johnson].

ALEXIS THACKET 21, female. The older sister of Emily Thacket, a missing teenager [Jess Jones].

LISA HARTNELL 30s, female. Matt's wife [Laurel Ullman].

TIME & SETTING

Present. A small town on the edge of a state park.

SCENE ONE

LIGHTS UP

On ALEXIS THACKET SITTING at a table in a small coffee house. She seems unsure, waiting. MATT HARTNELL WALKS over with two coffee cups. He has a folder tucked under his arm.

MATT Alexis?

[*She nods back.*]

MATT I'm Matt Hartnell.

[*Alexis RISES to shake his hand. He has to awkwardly shift the cups into one hand to do so.*]

MATT I wasn't sure if you liked tea or coffee, so I got both.

[*Alexis pauses before taking both. They sit. Matt eagerly pulls out the folder from under his arm and hands it to her.*]

MATT I wanted you to check some of my notes. I've got a timeline of the case here, and some thoughts on its developments.

[*Alexis takes a moment to peruse the papers.*]

MATT [*pointing to a section*] If you look here, I've tracked the time Emily got out of school. . . . two p.m. . . . .up to when a witness last saw her. . . . two forty-five. . . . leaving the square. Here's the list of suspects that we checked out the first week, and statements from her friends, here.

ALEXIS Wait. [*beat*] It's been three months. I thought you'd have more leads than this. Has anyone come forward?

[*Matt hesitates.*]

ALEXIS This town's so small, we have more trees than people. I don't want to keep going with false hope.

MATT I was hoping we'd be able to have a conversation about this.

ALEXIS I've been through everything already. Weren't you looking into that kid in her class?

MATT Well, if you look here. . . .

ALEXIS I can see that. But what else do you have?

MATT What about your parents? What have they told you?

ALEXIS Nothing. My mom's afraid of saying the wrong thing to anyone.

[*Matts pulls out a small pad of paper and is poised to write.*]

ALEXIS She didn't do it, so don't go there. She's scared the public will hate her if it gets out.

MATT If what gets out?

ALEXIS Police got suspicious after she told them about her fight with Emily three days before. You know how words get thrown around in arguments. You don't think about them till later, and you usually have the next day to apologize. [*beat*] This was a mistake. I shouldn't be saying anything.

[*She starts to gather her things.*]

MATT Wait.

[*He scribbles something on a piece of paper before ripping it off and handing it to her.*]

MATT My number. Please take it.

[*She does, hesitantly. Matt offers her the jacket. She slips into it. He watches with disappointment as she EXITS.*]

END OF SCENE

SCENE TWO

Matt's bedroom. Matt lies on the bed, watching a news broadcast. *The anchor is discussing Emily Thacket's disappearance.* The door opens and his wife, LISA, ENTERS. She is dressed in business attire.

MATT Hey, there. How was work?

LISA Oh, the usual.

[*She starts shedding her blazer. Matt, ever the gentleman, helps her out of it and neatly folds it.*]

LISA Can you look into getting a fence for the garden? Something's gnawing at the plants.

MATT Raccoons or something?

LISA That's my guess. I was thinking of ordering some takeout. That work for you tonight?

MATT Can't, need to leave for work soon.

LISA Well, waltz in there, throw down your badge, and tell them you'd rather have dinner with your wife.

MATT Yeah, that's going to work out well.

LISA Do you have the night shift tomorrow too?

MATT Yeah.

[*LIGHTS UP ON ANOTHER PART OF THE STAGE. Alexis APPEARS, puts her phone to her ear.*]

LISA Then let's have lunch.

MATT Sure.

[*Matt's PHONE RINGS. He checks the number. Lisa turns her attention to the TV broadcast.*]

LISA Anything new? It's awful, what they're doing. She's probably dead. Let the family have their peace.

MATT [*answering the phone*] Matt Hartnell.

ALEXIS It's Alexis Thacket.

MATT Hi.

ALEXIS It's on TV again. I can't escape it. [*beat*] Look, I'm sorry. . . . [*beat*] Can we meet? Same time tomorrow?

MATT Yeah, that's fine.

ALEXIS Okay. See you.

MATT Tomorrow.

ALEXIS Right.

MATT Bye.

[*He hangs up. Lisa gazes at him, curiously.*]

MATT Sorry, can't make lunch either. Josh needs a ride to the auto shop tomorrow. Got a problem with his tires.

[*He turns his attention back to the broadcast. Lisa moves closer to Matt, but his eyes aren't on her. Eventually, she gives up and EXITS.*]

END OF SCENE

SCENE THREE

Matt and Alexis at the coffee shop.

MATT Did Emily usually go straight home after school?

ALEXIS Sometimes she'd go to a friend's. Mom told me to lend her my phone charger before she left that morning. She always lost hers. But I slept in and never gave it to her.

[*Matt considers comforting her in some way, but can't bring himself to move his hand very far.*]

[*LIGHTS ON MATT AND LISA'S BEDROOM. Lisa ENTERS, looking for Matt. Disappointed, she sits on the bed, notices that he has left his phone behind.*]

ALEXIS It's not like she doesn't know the woods. She even camped out there once, I think, to piss off our parents.

[*Picking up Matt's phone, Lisa notes a phone number on the screen. After a curious beat, she presses "dial."*]

[*Alexis's PHONE RINGS.*]

ALEXIS Sorry, I'm used to leaving it on all the time now. [*turning it off*] I'll answer it later. [*beat*] I'm not sure what you want to hear.

MATT You don't have to say anything you don't want to.

[*OVER IN LISA AND MATT'S BEDROOM, Lisa listens as the call goes to VOICE MAIL.*]

VOICE MAIL [*recording, quick, cheerful*] "Not here, leave a message!"

ALEXIS Then why give me your number in the first place?

MATT Because no one talks to you.

[*Upset and near tears, Lisa EXITS the bedroom.*]

ALEXIS My parents didn't want me speaking to the police.

MATT Why?

ALEXIS My sister and I had a complicated relationship. Her room is right across from mine. If we had our doors open and I'd see her dancing to some music video, I'd make fun of her. She'd stick her tongue out then slam her door.

[*She stops, and starts to choke up. Matt fumbles for a tissue.*]

ALEXIS [*chuckling*] There were times when you didn't know if she'd hug you or slap you.

[*Matt RISES.*]

MATT I think that's good for today. We've been at it awhile. Let's save the rest for Thursday.

ALEXIS This can't be your first missing child. Does it ever work out?

[*He doesn't answer right away. Then he looks right at her, sad, but not pitying. He gives her the tissue.*]

MATT See you next week.

[*Alexis nods, takes the tissue and EXITS.*]

END OF SCENE

SCENE FOUR

Matt and Lisa's bedroom. Lisa is seated on the bed. A packed bag is on the floor next to her. Matt ENTERS.

MATT Hey.

[*He attempts to give her a kiss, but she keeps her eyes forward.*]

MATT I'm sorry. We always keep missing meals, huh? When was the last time we had a real date?

LISA A year ago. [*beat*] You forgot your phone. And I talked to Josh. He's out of town.

MATT I had to take an extra shift. I didn't want to tell you.

LISA Don't act like I'm not smart enough to figure this out.

MATT It was just for a few more hours. Nothing major.

[*Lisa reveals his phone and waves it angrily.*]

LISA Her number was on your phone!

[*She hands it back to him.*]

LISA She sounded young. God, I hope she's legal. [*giving him a cold stare*] Who is she?

MATT Alexis Thacket.

LISA [*horrified*] I wouldn't think you'd sink that low. Taking advantage of that poor girl.

MATT It's not like that. She needed to talk to someone.

LISA Why should you be the one?

MATT I understand her loss.

LISA *Her* loss? What about ours? We went through hell last year, trying to mourn, grieve, accept. I went three times a week for therapy. Not once did you offer to come, or even ask how it went. Right when I think I'm getting better, I lose my husband too?

MATT This is different.

LISA   Just because she's someone else's kid? It's like you're trying to forget what happened to our baby!

MATT   I didn't forget.

LISA   Then what are you doing?

MATT   Coping.

LISA   [*beat*] Well, try doing it alone.

[*Lisa shoulders her bag and EXITS.*]

END OF SCENE

SCENE FIVE

The coffee shop. ALEXIS ENTERS. MATT RISES to greet her.

ALEXIS   [*upset*] You weren't answering your phone, so I went over to the station. They don't have a Matt Hartnell on their force. But they knew one. They questioned you! [*beat*] You pull all this shit, you play detective, you trick me into reliving all of that! You knew I hated talking about it! What sick game were you playing? [*beat*] You're a park ranger! Why are you doing this?!

MATT   [*contrite beat*] To see if the police missed anything. I know these woods. I helped them the first few days.

ALEXIS   Helping by pointing them in the wrong direction? I read the reports. "Park Ranger saw girl near woods the day before her disappearance." [*beat*] How can you tell me you aren't involved? The police know about you, talked to you about it!

MATT   They questioned everyone even a little related to the case, including you.

ALEXIS   What did you see? What was she doing?

MATT   She slipped around the gate after dark. I let her off with a warning.

ALEXIS Why?

MATT Why was she out there? I don't know. You know her better. I kept looking around the area I first saw her. . . . the northeast corner, near the caves. Nothing. I checked all the way from the campgrounds to the bus station.

ALEXIS The bus station?

MATT [*brushing it off*] Yeah, it's way down at the south end of the park. I've covered nearly every acre. . . .

ALEXIS Didn't you look there?

MATT The bus station? No, it's out of my jurisdiction.

[*Alexis stands in silence for a few moments. She starts to leave, but hesitates. She turns back to him, as though to say something, but decides not to. She turns again, and EXITS.*]

END OF SCENE

SCENE SIX

Matt and Lisa's bedroom. Matt is seated on the bed, watching a news broadcast about a *break in the Emily Thacket case*. Lisa ENTERS. She sets down her bag, and sits on the opposite side of the bed.

MATT Didn't think you'd come back. [*beat*] They found her. . . . in New York.

LISA Kidnapped?

MATT Ran away. She was living on the streets. Alexis figured it out.

LISA But she's safe.

MATT Yeah. [*beat*] I have a hearing on Wednesday. Impersonating an officer.

LISA Think the charges will stick?

MATT I don't know. I hear Alexis vouched for me.

[*Lisa nods. Matt spots a corner of pink sticking out of Lisa's bag.*]

MATT Did you take that with you?

[*Lisa nods and slowly pulls out a PINK BABY BLANKET. Matt takes a corner of the blanket, rubs it gently between his fingers. Lisa takes the other end. As they sit, holding it together, they watch the news broadcast.*]

FADE TO BLACK

END OF PLAY

Pegging Out

BY BRONWEN CLARK

Copyright © by Bronwen Clark. All rights reserved. Published with permission from the author. Inquiries concerning rights should be addressed to Bronwen Clark at bronwenhclark@gmail.com.

Pegging Out

Presented October 25, 2013 | Kenan Theatre, UNC Department of Dramatic Art | Directed by Dana Coen

CHARACTERS

Original cast members are in brackets.

ALVIE 24, male. A working-class British miner, who seeks the approval of his older brother [Brandon Rafalson].

HARMON 33, male, Alvie's older brother. A working-class British miner. He has a broken leg and a racking cough [Ben Elling].

GIDEON 48, male. A lonely Welsh miner [Ian Bowater].

VOICE 30s, male. A member of the rescue team [Greg Hohn].

TIME & SETTING

Present. Inside a collapsed British coal mine.

SCENE ONE

IN THE BLACK, we first hear the SOUND OF STATIC, then the weary voice of ALVIE.

ALVIE This is Alvie Pugh. Down in Shaft C. Well, what was Shaft C. Over. [*beat, a BEEP*] There was a burst just past the break line. We've got a pretty bad roof sag. Do you copy? [*beat, another BEEP*] Is anybody on?

[*The rough voice of HARMON is heard.*]

HARMON There's no use dicking around with that thing, Alvie. There's no one near enough.

ALVIE I thought you were asleep.

HARMON Not with the racket you're making.

ALVIE Somebody's got to try, haven't they?

HARMON You might as well try ordering takeaway.

ALVIE I must have the wrong frequency. If I could just remember the right channel. . . .

HARMON There's no one coming for us! Just go to sleep, alright?

[*A CAP LAMP FLARES, revealing HARMON, slouched against a support beam. ALVIE is seated on a wheelbarrow, holding the TWO-WAY. Both are filthy and unshaven. Two backpacks, mining tools, and chunks of rock rest between them. Harmon shields his eyes.*]

HARMON For Chrissake, Alvie! Warn me next time! [*beat*] You're going to waste the battery.

ALVIE I just needed to see you.

[*Alvie RISES. Harmon drags himself into more of a reclining position, grasps his leg in pain.*]

ALVIE How long do you think we've been down here?

HARMON [*sarcastic*] A fortnight.

ALVIE Really? That long?

HARMON How the hell do I know? There's no sun, is there? How do you expect me to know how many days it's been?

ALVIE Days, then?

HARMON Yeah, probably. [*beat*] God only knows what Anne's thinking. . . . that she's scared me off, most likely.

ALVIE Scared you off?

HARMON You know, the baby?

ALVIE Oh. Right.

HARMON [*scoffing*] You've already forgotten?

ALVIE How's the leg?

HARMON Brilliant. I'll be fit for the fucking ballet next week.

[*Alvie bends to check it.*]

HARMON Don't touch it, you idiot! Piss off, would you?

ALVIE You need anything, then?

HARMON You've done enough.

[*Alvie rummages through a backpack.*]

ALVIE You want a biscuit? We've still got a bit left.

HARMON No.

ALVIE You've got to eat something.

HARMON What for? To keep my strength up for dying?

ALVIE No one's dying down here, Harm. Let me take care of you.

HARMON You can't even take care of yourself.

ALVIE It was an accident. I keep telling you.

HARMON You always go where you shouldn't. You always have, Alvie.

[*Alvie brings him a biscuit.*]

ALVIE Here. You get cranky when you're hungry.

HARMON [*chucking the biscuit away*] You always have to pester, don't you, Alvie? Can't you just leave me alone? Let me rest in peace!

[*A distant CRASH of rock is heard.*]

ALVIE What was that?

HARMON   Ground's just shifting.

[*A soft WHISTLING is heard. A LIGHT appears on ANOTHER PART OF THE STAGE and grows brighter.*]

ALVIE   Harmon, look! Look! Someone's coming! [*shouting*] Hey! Over here! Hey!

[*GIDEON APPEARS. He carries a lamp. His clothes are torn.*]

GIDEON   [*Welsh accent*] Aha! I knew I heard voices. You fellows all right? Damn tight spot you're in, yeah?

ALVIE   Harmon, I told you they were coming!

GIDEON   Been looking for you for days.

[*Gideon surveys their camp. Alvie gathers their belongings.*]

HARMON   How did you find us? The tunnels are all blocked.

GIDEON   Oh, I know every inch of this mountain. [*touching the wall fondly*] Nobody knows it better'n me.

[*Harmon cocks his head at Gideon.*]

HARMON   Don't think I've seen you before. You been working this mine?

GIDEON   I was on the other side.

HARMON   Yeah? Whose crew?

GIDEON   Porter's. Shaft A.

[*Alvie SHOULDERS a backpack and motions to Harmon.*]

ALVIE   My brother's leg. . . . he's not going to be able to walk very far. [*peering behind Gideon*] The others back there, then? Where's the rest of your crew?

GIDEON   Oh, in their beds, I s'pose. Maybe down at the pub. Bunch of drunk bastards. [*beat*] You fellows mind if I join you?

ALVIE   Join us? You're not getting us out of here?

GIDEON   Would if I could, mate. I'm trapped down here, as well. [*Gideon pulls out some cards.*] Name's Gideon, by the way. Fancy a game of cribbage?

[*Alvie and Harmon stare back with stunned surprise.*]

END OF SCENE

SCENE TWO

LATER. The lamp is on the floor. Gideon and Harmon are playing cards, using pebbles as pegs. Alvie has the two-way. We hear STATIC.

GIDEON   That's fifteen. Two points for me. Sorry, lad. Let's count up, shall we?

HARMON   What's a triple, again?

GIDEON   Triples are six. Pairs are two. Quadruples, twelve. Easy enough, yeah?

ALVIE   [*into the two-way*] Hello? Anyone on? Hello? Answer me, goddammit!

[*He hits the radio and shakes it.*]

GIDEON   Come have a round, Alvie. Take a break.

ALVIE   No. I'm not giving up.

HARMON   And I've got a flush with the cut. . . .

GIDEON   Cut can't give you a flush. It gives you the fifth if it's past a four-card flush, see? Didn't your Da ever teach you?

HARMON   [*throwing down his cards*] Wasn't around to.

ALVIE   This damn thing is useless. Where's yours, Gideon?

GIDEON   Broke a while back. [*to Harmon*] Don't worry. You'll get the hang of it. Can't learn it all in a few hours, can you? Took me ages to figure it out.

ALVIE We won't be here ages.

GIDEON They're bound to seal it off, lad. It's the economical thing to do, yeah? We're quite far down, you know. Easier for them to just board it up and carry on. Put it down as an accident.

ALVIE It was an accident. It was dark.

[*Alvie kicks a rock. Gideon shuffles the cards.*]

HARMON I told him not to go down this way. Didn't listen. Never does.

GIDEON Signs get covered in dust. Hard to read. Light down here's awful, too. Taken many a wrong turn myself.

HARMON Yeah, but Alvie takes nothing but wrong turns.

[*Gideon SHUFFLES away.*]

GIDEON What's done is done, yeah? Can't do anything about it now. Fancy another round? Alvie?

[*Alvie considers, then slowly crosses back, sits down.*]

GIDEON Good lad.

END OF SCENE

SCENE THREE

LATER. Gideon and Alvie are playing. Harmon wears the cap lamp to illuminate a note he's writing on a scrap of paper. Alvie lets out a WHOOP and flourishes his cards happily.

ALVIE Ha! Look at that!

GIDEON I haven't been beat in years. You've pegged out!

ALVIE Beginner's luck, yeah?

GIDEON No, you're a natural.

[*Alvie grins and reaches for a pack.*]

ALVIE You hungry, Gid? I could eat a horse. Want a biscuit?

GIDEON Haven't a taste for them.

ALVIE Just as well. Only got a couple left. Stale, of course.

[*The cap lamp DIMS.*]

HARMON Damn. Bring me that lamp, Alvie, would you?

[*Alvie sets Gideon's lamp beside Harmon. He peeks at the paper.*]

ALVIE What are you scribbling?

HARMON Nothing.

[*Alvie reads over Harmon's shoulder.*]

ALVIE What's this about a mason jar?

[*Harmon shields the paper.*]

HARMON Piss off, Alvie!

ALVIE You writing a letter to Anne?

HARMON Last will and testament, more like. I want her to know where I kept my winnings.

ALVIE Under the floorboard, beneath the piano.

HARMON You know where it is?

ALVIE It's not that good a hiding spot.

HARMON You've probably gone in there to get a shilling for a pint, haven't you?

ALVIE I wouldn't touch that money, Harm! I swear I wouldn't.

[*Gideon holds up a hand.*]

GIDEON Easy, easy. What's it matter now, lads? Whole lot of good it'll do you, arguing about it down here.

HARMON It's not much, anyway. Hardly enough for a crib. You know, I could've made her a crib. Probably the only good I could've done, anyway.

ALVIE When we get out of here, we'll make a crib together.

[*Harmon snorts. A long silence.*]

HARMON It doesn't matter if you're waiting for rescue or waiting to die. It's the waiting that's the hardest part. I just wish it would happen quick.

[*Gideon STANDS AND PACES. He looks up at the ceiling.*]

GIDEON [*reflective*] I was waiting for the rocks to fall. I remember. . . . I was sure they were going to crush me, that they were going to shatter my bones into a million pieces. It was deeper than they thought, the shaft. They were just having a bit of fun. I called for help, but they all just disappeared. So, I kept waiting. They told the shift boss I'd been fooling around where I shouldn't've been. Sealed it without bothering to get my body. There was no one to claim it, anyway.

[*A long beat as Harmon gapes at Gideon.*]

HARMON [*shocked*] Holy hell. Holy hell!

[*Harmon SCRAMBLES away from him.*]

GIDEON It's all right!

[*Alvie, curious, circles Gideon. Gideon lets Alvie examine him. Alvie touches his face, his shoulders, his hands.*]

HARMON Get away from him, Alvie! Don't. . . .

[*The two-way SCREECHES. Alvie continues to stare at Gideon.*]

VOICE ON TWO-WAY Hello? Hello, can anyone hear me? Are you there? Over.

[*Harmon lunges for the two-way. Gideon grips Alvie's hand. Alvie doesn't recoil.*]

HARMON Yes, yes, hello? We're here, we're here! This is Harmon Pugh. We're here! Yes! Hello? Over?

[*Alvie places his hand over Gideon's. A look of understanding passes between them.*]

VOICE ON TWO-WAY Fucking hell, Harmon. Can you hold out a bit longer? We're edging down the shaft now. Almost near enough to drill. We'll keep you posted. Over.

HARMON Almost near enough. Almost near enough, Alvie! [*to Gideon*] You, don't come near me! Go on, won't you!

ALVIE Easy, Harm. He's not hurting you, none.

HARMON Just stay away from me.

[*Distant ECHO OF A HAMMERING DRILL.*]

HARMON You hear that? They're coming! Alvie, you were right, for once! How about that?

[*Harmon crumples up the paper in excitement.*]

ALVIE What have you been doing down here, Gid, all alone.

[*Gideon fondly touches the wall. Harmon STRUGGLES TO STAND.*]

GIDEON There's a bit to see, you know. Tunnels and shafts that have been blocked for decades.

ALVIE Yeah?

HARMON Give me a hand, Alvie!

[*Alvie ignores him.*]

GIDEON There's a haulage way just below here that leads to another drift. It goes all the way down to the sump. I reckon I'm the only one's been down there in years. It's a sight. All that water. Still as death. It's peaceful, there. The air is different. Like there's no pressure to it.

[*Harmon reaches out a hand to Alvie.*]

HARMON Help me up, Alvie! I can't do this by myself!

ALVIE There's a whole world down here, isn't there?

GIDEON Places I haven't even explored, yet. There's always something to see, something to do.

HARMON Alvie!

[*The sound of a DRILL gets closer. The SOUND OF ROCKS CLATTERING around them. They all look up. Harmon pants and leans against the wall.*]

HARMON They're almost here!

[*Alvie takes a step toward Gideon.*]

ALVIE You know, I think I'd like to see that sump.

GIDEON It's a bit of a trek. I don't know if you'd be back in time.

[*Alvie shrugs. (beat) Gideon grins.*]

GIDEON Right this way, lad. You'll have to crawl a bit, I'm afraid, but there's room to walk just around the bend. Just follow the light.

[*Gideon WALKS off. HIS LIGHT SLOWLY FADES. Harmon clutches the radio to his ear. Alvie takes one last look at him, then begins to FOLLOW Gideon.*]

HARMON [*into the radio*] Careful on the back.... it's hardly holding.... Alvie! Don't be running off, now! You can't go down there!

[*Alvie looks over his shoulder.*]

ALVIE You don't have to look after me anymore, Harm.

HARMON What do you mean?

[*A SCRAPING above. Dust falls.*]

ALVIE You can have that old room back. Turn it into a nursery.

[*Alvie takes a step, stops, and turns around for one last look at Harmon.*]

ALVIE There's an old Glengettie tin in the cupboard. Underneath the towels. I've been trying to save a bit, like you. I want you to have it, Harmon. And, don't worry. You'll be a great dad.

[*Alvie EXITS.*]

HARMON [*panicked*] Alvie!

[*The light FADES COMPLETELY. A sudden CRASH of rocks. A SHAFT OF LIGHT pierces the stage from above. Harmon looks up, CRIES OUT with a mixture of relief and grief. As he waits for his rescuers, two WHISTLERS are heard in the distance.*]

FADE TO BLACK

END OF PLAY

The Split

BY BRYANT CLEMENTS

Copyright © by Bryant Clements. All rights reserved. Published with permission from the author. Inquiries concerning rights should be addressed to Bryant Clements at bclements1091@gmail.com.

The Split

Presented October 25, 2013 | Kenan Theatre, UNC Department of Dramatic Art | Directed by Serena Ebhardt

CHARACTERS

Original cast members are in brackets.

JASPER ATKINSON 27, male, discontented [Brandon Rafalson].

GEORGE 29, male, chubby, nurturing [Ben Elling].

ADAM 28, male, dark and cynical [Max Cullen].

DETECTIVE PRICE 40s, male, experienced [Trevor Johnson].

TIME & SETTING

Present. New York City.

LIGHTS UP

On JASPER'S small one-bedroom apartment. The unit is cramped, bordering on messy and unkempt. JASPER ATKINSON ENTERS through the front door, looking fatigued. He carries a storage box filled to the brim with odds and ends. He sets the box down on a kitchen table and immediately pours himself a drink, pacing pensively as he sips. He starts searching through the objects in the box. He pulls out a fist-sized rock, pausing for a moment to stare at it. Jasper grabs a cloth from the table and begins scrubbing it. The task is interrupted when GEORGE ENTERS from another room. He is wearing khaki shorts and a brightly colored polo shirt. His rotund and friendly face is complemented by his chubby build.

GEORGE Whatup, Buttercup, how was dinner with Marcy?

[*The jovial greeting startles Jasper. He pauses, collects himself.*]

JASPER 'Twas fantastic. She actually enjoyed it so much that she asked me to take all my shit from her place and never see her again.

[*He gestures at the box. George looks at it pensively, then attempts to embrace Jasper in a bear hug. Jasper evades.*]

GEORGE Jasper, I'm so sorry, what happened?

JASPER I feel like I made it pretty clear.

GEORGE Quit with the fresh mouth, I need details! How else am I supposed to help you through this?

JASPER I don't know what else to say. She was just tired of dealing with me, I guess.

GEORGE I'm not buying it. From what I know about this girl she had to have given you a laundry list of reasons, so out with it! It'll be cathartic.

JASPER Detached, uncommitted, erratic.... all pretty standard fare for a breakup. I think she's been seeing someone else.

GEORGE Did she tell you that?

JASPER No, but she seemed all too pleased, like she couldn't wait to graze in greener pastures. She even tried to update her Facebook's relationship status in front of me right after she did the deed.

GEORGE Well, that is how you make it official. Everyone knows that. This is all just ignorance on her part. Pretty soon she'll be begging you to get back together.

JASPER Doubtful, things seemed pretty final. We were together too long anyway.

GEORGE It was six months. A mere drop in the vast pool of emotion that is our friendship.

JASPER You're next on the chopping block if you don't stop with all the questions. I don't really feel like talking about it.

GEORGE We both know I wouldn't be here if you didn't want me to. It's my duty to pester. I, at least, would like to know where she dropped the bomb.

JASPER Fair enough. Battery Park.

GEORGE That heartless bitch! Ending it where it all began! She wanted to make it sting. Your distant and erratic behavior must've pissed her off something fierce.

JASPER So it would appear. Had the good fortune of getting to go back to her place to get my stuff, though. Awkward breakup packing's good for the soul.

[*George looks over Jasper's shoulders as he peruses the box.*]

GEORGE You really settled in over there.

JASPER Unfortunately.

GEORGE Call me Mr. Brightside, but at least you'll be around here more now that Marcy's out of the picture. Hardly ever saw you when you two were together.

JASPER Yet another set of unfortunate circumstances.

[*George hesitates, choosing his words carefully.*]

GEORGE Rude. But I'm fine being your emotional punching bag, given the recent heartbreak.

[*Jasper stares at the fist-sized stone, tossing it between his hands.*]

GEORGE Whatcha got there? A nice metamorphic? Igneous?

JASPER [*agitated*] Nothing, just something stupid from Marcy.... a Pet Rock.

[*ADAM ENTERS from the other room, yawning and scratching his head.*]

GEORGE Ah, look who showed up! You're just in time. Don't worry. I'll fill you in.

JASPER [*to Adam*] There's no use trying to stop him. He won't shut up.

GEORGE [*frantic*] Jasper got home from having dinner with Marcy with that big box in his hands. I caught him out here looking super sad, sifting through his junk and. . . .

ADAM [*interrupting, coarse*] Yeah, yeah, I got it. Thin walls, loud, obnoxious voice. So how'd you fuck it up, you mutt?

JASPER I appreciate the words of encouragement, but I'm fine.

GEORGE He's actually torn up about it. He just doesn't know how to handle his emotions. I was just getting through that steely exterior when you decided to show up.

[*Adam approaches Jasper.*]

ADAM Look, build a bridge and get over it. The two of you were completely wrong for each other. Plus, she was a total bitch, always bossing you around and shit.

GEORGE [*to Adam*] You hush, she was great for him!

[*Adam points to the rock in Jasper's hands.*]

ADAM Case in point, that was her birthday gift to him. The most useless fuckin' thing on the planet.

GEORGE Pet Rock. Classic. Maybe it was her way of poking fun at your attachment issues, a steadfast companion that requires no effort, love, or care. Kind of like me!

ADAM Or maybe it's her way of giving a cheap-ass gift. Not even a name brand in a box, just a stray from her building's garden.

[*George goes in for a closer look at the rock.*]

GEORGE How is it missing an eye? You managed to maim a rock. Kudos to you, mon frère.

JASPER Keep pestering and I'll be happy to demonstrate.

[*Jasper drops the rock and EXITS the room. An AWKWARD SILENCE between the two follows. Jasper soon returns with a backpack. He starts placing some of the items from the box into it.*]

ADAM Just going to say one more thing and then I'll let it go, like George here should do. A girl like Marcy is a dime a dozen, easily replaceable. You need to get back out there and have some fun. I don't want to see you sitting around here, getting reacquainted with your right hand and Netflixing "Dr. Who."

GEORGE Sage advice. Leave It to Beaver and V.D. to get you back on your feet. Don't listen to me. . . . who even talks about their emotions nowadays?

ADAM Jesus, George! Will you shut the hell up?

GEORGE Sorry for trying to actually get him through this. Repressing it won't help anything. Outside of us, she was everything to him! He doesn't need us.

[*Jasper EXITS again, and quickly returns with some of his own clothes in his arms. He puts them in the backpack.*]

GEORGE [*excitedly*] Are we going on vacation?!

JASPER Not exactly. And I sure as hell wouldn't be taking you if I were.

GEORGE Marcy's gone. You're clearly not in a state to be alone. I'll get my resort wear.

ADAM You need another drink. A good brain bleaching always starts with copious amounts of alcohol.

JASPER Yeah, I could use another, actually.

[*Jasper grabs the bottle and ushers the two into the chairs. He procures three glasses and pours some into each glass.*]

GEORGE Drowning your problems in a sea of cheap liquor won't help.

[*Jasper quickly polishes off his.*]

ADAM He uses booze. You choose the pathetic path paved with pastries and self-pity. Goal's the same, just Jasper's hangover won't be over his belt.

[*George looks momentarily depressed, quickly glancing at his waistline and then strengthening his emotions.*]

GEORGE Simply a physical manifestation of my happiness. Say the word and I can whip up a Bundt cake quicker than Marcy dumped your broke ass.

[*George looks pleased with his sassy retort, only to find Jasper and Adam taking offense.*]

GEORGE Sorry, not helping. Little harsh, I guess. I'm done prying, but when you're ready to talk about whatever's on your mind, I'm here. . . . as always.

[*Jasper fills his glass again.*]

ADAM Finally, you'll let it go!

GEORGE I don't really see any other choice. You seem to have it all under control.

JASPER There's nothing to control, I'm fine. You know what? I'd actually love some cake, go. . . . do that.

GEORGE Might actually be better if you got out. Could do you some good to get some air. Human interaction. . . . clearly there's only so much we can do.

[*Jasper finishes his drink, SLAMMING the glass on the table.*]

JASPER Is that what you think? Do you really want to know the truth? I'm happy to spill. It doesn't take a shrink to tell me how fucked up....

[*A KNOCK on the door interrupts Jasper's outburst. The room goes silent. Jasper sits frozen for a beat. Another litany of KNOCKS is met by Jasper quickly grabbing his backpack and box and leaving the room. He comes back in without the items and answers the door, revealing DETECTIVE PRICE.*]

DETECTIVE PRICE Jasper Atkinson?

JASPER Yeah, that's me.

DETECTIVE PRICE Pardon me for coming by so late. My name's Detective Price. Mind if I come in for a moment?

[*Detective Price flashes his badge.*]

GEORGE Oh, it's the constable. How exciting!

[*George's comment goes unnoticed by Detective Price.*]

JASPER Uh, is there something I can help you with?

DETECTIVE PRICE Just need to talk to you, ask a few questions. Shouldn't take too long. Can I come in?

[*Jasper gives a disconcerted nod and moves out of the doorway. Detective Price ENTERS the apartment, carefully scanning his surroundings as he enters. Adam and George stand next to Jasper, spectating.*]

DETECTIVE PRICE Thanks, I appreciate your cooperation. Mind just telling me what you've been up to tonight?

JASPER Um, nothing too eventful, went to dinner with my girlfriend, just came back here afterwards. Is everything all right?

DETECTIVE PRICE Your girlfriend is Marcy Nicholson, correct?

JASPER Yeah, can you please just tell me what this is about? I'll be able to help more with whatever this is if I know what's going on.

DETECTIVE PRICE Was everything okay between the two of you tonight? Anything strange or out of the ordinary?

JASPER [*slightly frustrated*] Yeah, everything was good. But you showing up here is making me think otherwise.

[*Detective Price looks around the apartment.*]

ADAM [*to Jasper*] What are you doing? He probably already knows she broke up with you.

GEORGE Facebook "o-fish," the whole world knows.

[*Jasper gives an irritated glance at his critics.*]

DETECTIVE PRICE Were you at Ms. Nicholson's apartment this evening?

JASPER No, we both just went home after dinner. She's been really stressed at work lately, needed some sleep. Why are you asking me all of this?

[*George looks shocked at the lie.*]

DETECTIVE PRICE Ms. Nicholson was found unconscious in her apartment earlier this evening, as part of our invest....

JASPER [*interrupting*] Oh my God, is she okay? Where is she? I have to see her.

DETECTIVE PRICE Not at liberty to say.

JASPER Why not? Can you at least tell me what happened?

DETECTIVE PRICE The investigation's just getting started. I can't give out many details, but looks like blunt trauma to the head.

JASPER What do you mean.... like she was attacked?

[*Jasper BREAKS DOWN for a moment. Adam ponders this, connecting the dots.*]

DETECTIVE PRICE She's currently in a coma. Doctors are doing everything they can.

ADAM [*to Jasper*] Going to have to at least muster a tear.

DETECTIVE PRICE Can you give me any more information about what happened after you left dinner?

GEORGE [*to Adam, concerned*] What's he talking about?

[*Jasper is frozen, rubs his eyes in frustration.*]

ADAM Just sloppy work, could've at least finished the job.

GEORGE [*to Jasper*] Is this true? You have to tell the truth!

ADAM [*continuing*] .... Or gone for the emotional assault, ruined her for everyone else.

DETECTIVE PRICE Mr. Atkinson, are you all right?

[*Jasper regains focus.*]

JASPER Yeah, sorry, just a lot running through my head right now. We walked around Battery Park for a bit after dinner. As far as I know, she went home after we parted ways.

DETECTIVE PRICE Do you live here alone?

[*Detective Price points to the three glasses on the table.*]

JASPER Yeah, had a couple friends over earlier.

DETECTIVE PRICE Would you mind writing down their names and numbers for me?

[*He hands Jasper a notepad. Adam and George observe as he writes.*]

GEORGE [*re: notepad*] Who the hell are these guys?

JASPER Marcy's been talking about a guy at work who's borderline obsessed with her. Think he could've done this? I'll give you his info, too. She's seen him around her building a couple times.

DETECTIVE PRICE Would you come down to the station to give an official statement?

JASPER [*irritated*] Are you considering me a suspect? I don't even know what's going on. I think it's best if I don't say anything else till I get a lawyer.

ADAM Risky move, lawyer's a watermark of the guilty.

DETECTIVE PRICE That's your prerogative, but I'm going to have to insist you come to the station. Your cooperation will help us find out what happened to Ms. Nicholson.

JASPER [*panicked*] Are you arresting me?

ADAM He's been playing you this whole time.

DETECTIVE PRICE We need a formal statement. You can wait for your lawyer, or just go ahead and tell us where you really went on this evening. Choice is yours.

GEORGE Save everyone the trouble, Jasper.

ADAM He's bluffing.

GEORGE He obviously knows.

ADAM Don't say another word.

[*Jasper turns to them.*]

JASPER [*exploding*] God, just SHUT UP!

DETECTIVE PRICE Excuse me?

JASPER [*stammering*] I'm sorry. . . .

[*Everything goes silent. Jasper looks exasperated, confused.*]

DETECTIVE PRICE Why don't you come with me? I think I can help sort all this out.

[*A beat. Detective Price gently escorts Jasper from the apartment. Adam and George follow solemnly. The STAGE LIGHTS FADE OUT as a SPOTLIGHT illuminates the table where the glasses sit. . . . One is empty. The remaining two are untouched.*]

THE SPOTLIGHT FADES OUT

END OF PLAY

Hold Onto Me

BY JESSICA FILLHABER

Copyright © by Jessica Fillhaber. All rights reserved. Published with permission from the author. Inquiries concerning rights should be addressed to Jessica Fillhaber at jfillhaber@gmail.com.

Hold Onto Me

Presented October 25, 2013 | Kenan Theatre, UNC Department of Dramatic Art | Directed by Joseph Megel

CHARACTERS

Original cast members are in brackets.

SAM WISER 50, male. An investment advisor, competitive, stubborn, more sensitive than he appears [John Paul Middlesworth].

CORIN WISER 47, female. A loving yet smothering spouse, has OCD, constantly worries [Elisabeth Lewis Corley].

ROBERT SINGER 48, male. An investment advisor, easygoing, conscientious, level-headed [Greg Hohn].

TIME & SETTING

Fall, 2001. Sam and Corin's apartment in New York City, St. Vincent's Hospital-Manhattan.

SCENE ONE

LIGHTS UP

On SAM WISER and CORIN WISER. They lie stiffly in bed. CORIN's side of the room is neat, while SAM's side is untidy with piles of clothes strewn about the floor. As SAM moves to get out of bed, CORIN attempts to follow. SAM stops her with his arm.

SAM It's fine. Stay in bed.

CORIN Let me make you. . . .

SAM I'm not hungry.

[*Sam sits at the edge of the bed. He puts his head down, massaging it with his hands. Corin RISES from the bed, retrieves a button-down shirt from off the floor and places it on her ironing board. She clicks the dial on the iron THREE times, then quickly presses it. Meanwhile, Sam picks a plain white shirt from the top of a pile on the floor and puts it on. Corin brings the pressed shirt over and hands it to Sam.*]

CORIN Here, sweetie.

SAM This shirt's good.

[*Corin tries to kiss him on the lips, but he gives her his cheek.*]

CORIN [*recovering*] I went out yesterday and got more eggs. Want me to make your favorite?

SAM No.

CORIN [*dejected*] Maybe tomorrow then.

[*Sam sits back down on the bed and stares into space. Corin walks over to the closet and opens it. She chooses a dress and closes the door, touching it THREE times.*]

SAM [*quietly*] Still doing that, I see.

CORIN [*putting on the dress and slipping into a pair of shoes*] What was that?

SAM [*louder, annoyed*] I said, I see you're still doing that. Don't you know there are better ways to spend the day than counting and touching and pushing and arranging and rearranging everything all the God damn time?

CORIN Please, Sam, just let me be. We all handle things in our own way.

SAM No, Corin, this is getting to be ridiculous. There's so much going on in this world that deserves attention. Why don't you make a contribution to something?

CORIN If we're going to talk about things we could improve, why don't you take a shower? How many days has it been?

SAM So, now you're my mother?

CORIN Well, while I'm at it, you have that appointment today with Dr. Parsons. If you won't shower for me, at least do it for her.

SAM I think I'll just save both of us the trouble and not go.

CORIN [*trying to be gentle*] This will be the third time you've cancelled this week. You have to go.

SAM They can keep our damn money! Paying someone to simply talk to you isn't even a real profession! It's a waste of time.

CORIN I don't und....

SAM Just please, let me be.

[*Corin CROSSES to Sam's side of the bed. He watches her, as if he knows what's coming next. She bends down to pick up a pair of his jeans off of the floor.*]

SAM I'll get that.

CORIN Yeah? When? [*no response*] I need to do a few things at the office. You'll be all right?

[*Sam pulls on the pair of jeans.*]

SAM I'll manage.

[*Corin starts to leave, but turns back around.*]

CORIN I hate it when we fight. That's all we do lately. [*sighing after no response*] Alright, I'll be home later. If you think of something you want for dinner, call me and I'll get it on my way back.

[*Corin EXITS and closes the door behind her. Sam watches as the knob turns THREE times on the inside.*]

END OF SCENE

SCENE TWO

NIGHT. Sam and Corin's apartment. Sam sits in front of the television. Corin ENTERS. Sam doesn't look up. She CROSSES over and stands behind him.

CORIN Why are you watching that, sweetie? [*no answer*] I just think it will make things worse. Why don't you put on something else?

[*Corin reaches for the remote, but Sam stops her.*]

SAM I'll make a deal with you. I'll stop watching when you stop with your compulsions.

CORIN [*upset*] I slave all day, making sure everything is just right for you. I do the laundry, cook, clean, make the plans, go to work, everything. But you don't notice it, notice me.

SAM Well, at least you get to go to work! [*RISING*] I have to get out of here.

[*Sam CROSSES to the door and SLAMS it as he EXITS.*]

END OF SCENE

SCENE THREE

ROBERT SINGER lies in a hospital bed, reading. One of his legs has been amputated. Sam appears at the door, KNOCKS.

SAM Hey. I. . . . uh. . . . didn't mean to interrupt, so I can just come back later if that would be better. I was just, you know, walking around, and I guess I ended up here.

ROBERT You shouldn't be doing that. It's not good to breathe in too much of that air, you know. Come in. I've been waiting for you to show up.

SAM [*uneasily*] How are you doing?

ROBERT Breathing.

SAM Yeah. [*beat*] How's your progress?

ROBERT They tell me I'll be walking in no time. Just waiting on the prosthetic. Doctor says I'm a miracle.

SAM Nothing feels magical about this.

[*Sam sits.*]

ROBERT Go ahead, say it.

SAM Say what?

ROBERT You know.

SAM [*frustrated*] I didn't come here to talk to you in ambiguities. . . .

ROBERT Yes, so why did you come?

[*Sam is silent for a moment. He looks around, fiddles with his hands. Robert waits patiently.*]

SAM [*quietly*] Why did you go back in?

ROBERT Hmm?

SAM [*louder*] I said, why did you go back in?

ROBERT Why does it matter?

SAM You know, I've been getting a lot more questions than answers lately. If I could just get one God damn answer, that would be great.

ROBERT Yeah, that *would* be great.

SAM [*RISES, begins gesticulating*] We spent over two decades in that building. Now it's all dust. Aren't you angry? Aren't you angry at everyone, at everything? Don't you think about what would have happened if you'd called in sick that morning? Don't you wonder why you, why me? I could have helped. I should have gone back in with you.

ROBERT Yeah, and you could be in this bed with one leg, too.

[*Sam looks uncomfortable. Robert softens.*]

SAM Rob, you're a hero. I'm nothing. Tell me! Why was I there?

ROBERT I don't know. Maybe because you worked there. You got up like you did every morning, just like thousands of other people. It was chaos. You know; you saw it. People were everywhere, running towards it, running away from it. You can't think clearly in a situation like that. I tried leaving. Twice, actually. I'm not a hero, Sam. We just made different choices in that second. People did lots of things that day.

SAM But that doesn't change the fact that I was one of the people who did NOTHING! Sometimes I can't breathe....

ROBERT [*getting angry*] I didn't do much either, okay?

SAM What are you talking about?

ROBERT The ceiling caved and fell on my leg before I was able to get to anyone.

SAM What?

ROBERT Nothing is different because I went back. Don't you see?

SAM But you tried.

ROBERT And failed! I was just another body that needed to be pulled out.

SAM But Rob....

ROBERT There are no buts. I'm here.... with one leg. That's all there is.

SAM I don't know what to say.

ROBERT Me neither. [*beat*] It's late, you should go home. Corin must be worried sick.

SAM [*dazed*] I'm sorry, Robert.

ROBERT Yeah, me too.

SAM I'll see you.

ROBERT You know where to find me.

[*Sam nods, EXITS.*]

END OF SCENE

SCENE FOUR

Corin and Sam's apartment. Corin is in bed. Sam quietly opens the door and SHUFFLES IN. Walking over to the bed, he takes off his shirt and pants and places them neatly on top of his dresser. He gets into bed and lies there rigidly for a moment. Corin turns over and looks at him.

CORIN [*quietly, gently*] Hi.

SAM Hi.

[*After a moment, Corin slowly moves her hand to gingerly touch Sam's. Sam holds his hand there limply for a moment, and then grabs on tightly. He brings her hand to his chest and gently TAPS HER HAND THREE TIMES. She sighs gently and closes her eyes.*]

FADE TO BLACK

END OF PLAY

Knives Make It Personal

BY HANNAH FLOYD

Copyright © by Hannah Floyd. All rights reserved. Published with permission from the author. Inquiries concerning rights should be addressed to Hannah Floyd at hfloyd@ad.unc.edu.

Knives Make It Personal

Premiered November 15, 2012 | Swain Hall, Studio 6 Theatre, UNC Department of Communication | Directed by Leslie Cloninger

CHARACTERS

Original cast members are in brackets.

CELIA 20s, female, attractive. The actress playing Henry's boss YATES [Samantha Hawkins].

LEWIS 20s, male, likeable smile. The actor playing HENRY, a man who kills his boss [Cressler Peele].

THE DIRECTOR 30s, male. He's high-strung, short-tempered, egocentric [Leslie Cloninger].

KENNY 20s, male. An anxious playwright, takes himself seriously, spends too much time indoors [Christian Payne].

TIME & SETTING

Present. A business office stage set.

LIGHTS UP

On an office set. CELIA [as the character YATES], dressed in business attire, sits at a desk, talking on the phone.

CELIA [*as YATES*] Uh huh. . . . Yeah. . . . I see. Yes, I'll need those figures by the end of the week.

[*As she speaks, a nervous-looking LEWIS, as the character HENRY, APPROACHES from behind, stops to wipe sweat off of his forehead.*]

CELIA [*as YATES, into phone*] Yes, I understand, Bill. I do. It's a numbers game. You know that.

[*Lewis, as HENRY, looms eerily over Celia. He pulls a KNIFE out of his pocket. His hand shakes.*]

CELIA [*as YATES, into phone*] Yes. Yes, I'll call him in here. Hang on a minute. HENRY!

[*She swivels in her chair. Lewis, as HENRY, PAUSES before he PLUNGES the knife into her chest. She SLUMPS OVER in her chair, FALLING onto her desk. He stares at the slumped body for a moment. Then, breaking character....*]

LEWIS Any better that time?

[*THE DIRECTOR APPROACHES.*]

DIRECTOR To be honest, Lew? No. You keep pausing before you stab her.

LEWIS Are you sure? I didn't think I was.

DIRECTOR In the time it takes you to do it, she can run across the street!

LEWIS Well, I can try again.

DIRECTOR This is the scene where Henry loses it. He's so overcome with rage and passion that he finally does it; he finally kills his boss. He doesn't pause to stop and think about it. Tell me, why does Henry use a knife instead of a gun?

LEWIS Uh, practicality? Guns are loud?

DIRECTOR Practicality? [*scoffing*] Guns are cold and automatic, but knives, knives are emotion and boiling blood! Knives make it personal. Henry hates his boss, and he hates her deeply. Personally.

[*He shakes his head, exasperated.*]

LEWIS I guess on some level I just can't imagine Henry actually killing his boss. It just feels so inconsistent with his character.

DIRECTOR [*calling offstage*] Hey, Kenny? Kenny, could you come in here for a second, please?

[*The disheveled playwright KENNY ENTERS. He holds a notebook in his hand and nervously chews a pencil.*]

DIRECTOR [*to Lewis*] Could you repeat what you just said?

LEWIS [*quietly*] It's just that Henry doesn't feel like much of a killer.

DIRECTOR [*to Kenny*] Go ahead. Chekhov him.

KENNY The playwright Anton Chekhov said, "If you say in the first chapter that there is a rifle hanging on the wall, in the second or third chapter, it ABSOLUTELY must go off! If it's not going to be fired, it shouldn't be there!"

DIRECTOR Basic plant and payoff.

[*Lewis looks confused.*]

KENNY Throughout the whole script I have Henry playing around with this knife. If she doesn't die in the last scene, the whole thing falls apart. It's Theater 101.

DIRECTOR [*to Lewis*] So basically, this is the most important scene in the play, which means you have to become capable of killing your boss, this person [*motioning to Celia*] by the end of rehearsal, or else the producers and I will be having yet another discussion about casting popular actors in roles they aren't right for regardless of how much everyone loves them.

LEWIS [*sadly*] Right.

[*Lewis slumps away and takes a seat on a bench. As Celia turns to cross away. . . .*]

DIRECTOR One moment, Celia.

[*Celia turns back.*]

DIRECTOR Okay, I have an idea: You need to piss him off. . . . you, personally.

CELIA Lewis? He's like the nicest guy in the. . . .

DIRECTOR Yes, yes, so they've told me. But, manipulation is my business. And last I checked, acting was yours. So act. In order for Lewis to become his character, you have to become more like yours. You've got to get under his skin.

CELIA How do I do that?

DIRECTOR Do what Yates does. Try to make him feel inferior, demean him a little if you have to. It's for his own good. You two take a few minutes alone while I chat with Kenny.

[*Kenny and The Director EXIT. Celia takes a moment before joining Lewis on the bench.*]

CELIA Lewis? Can I talk to you for a moment?

LEWIS Of course.

CELIA I'm frustrated with you. As long as you keep fudging the kill, no one's going to notice my performance. You're blowing the scene!

LEWIS Yeah, I know. I'm sorry. It's a shame. You are really amazing at dying.

CELIA [*taken aback*] Well, I do have some impressive credentials behind me. I mean, I guess we should hope so, right? Seeing as I'm the star.

LEWIS I know Henry's the protagonist, and he gets a lot more stage time, but I've always felt the same way. Yates is the real star. It's her play.

CELIA [*trudging onward*] I'm not sure it was written that way. I think it was actually the director's vision. . . .

[*Impressed, Lewis pulls out a small NOTEBOOK and begins taking notes.*]

CELIA He cast me as Yates because he wanted her to shine, and that's why, for the part of Henry, he chose someone with such. . . . well, limited range.

LEWIS To tell you the truth, Celia, that's part of the reason I auditioned for the play in the first place. . . . to have the chance to work with you. But I guess your talent isn't rubbing off on me as much as I'd hoped.

[*The Director APPROACHES.*]

DIRECTOR Celia, a word?

[*Celia CROSSES to The Director.*]

DIRECTOR [*out of Lewis's earshot*] How's it going?

CELIA I don't think it's working. [*beat*] Some people were just born nice.

DIRECTOR Doesn't mean they have to stay that way. I have another idea. Maybe pissing him off a little isn't thinking big enough. Maybe you have to make him really hate you, the way Yates makes Henry hate her. By insulting him deeply, personally, by making him question himself as a man. I happen to know that oversized heart of his was recently broken. He tried to pull that as an excuse earlier. So jump in there and twist the knife.

CELIA That seems so cruel. . . . and manipulative.

DIRECTOR [*shrugs*] Theater, baby.

[*The Director EXITS. Celia walks back over to Lewis. They take a seat on the bench.*]

CELIA So, I heard Laura dumped you.

LEWIS Yeah. Right out of the blue. [*smiling sadly at her*] Thanks for checking up on me. Really, it means a lot.

CELIA Out of the blue, huh? It was probably on account of your salary, right? She wanted more of a real man, someone who could provide for her.

LEWIS God, that's incredible. How'd you know?! Well, I guess you're an actor, too, right? So you understand.

[*He gazes at her compassionately.*]

CELIA I mean, it had to be more than that, though. [*feigning sympathy*] Did it bother her that you're.... well.... I'll just say it.... a little effeminate. Was that it?

LEWIS [*amazed*] You have, like.... insight superpowers! I mean, let's face it, as an actor, I have to be emotional. Wearing our feelings on our sleeves is part of our job description. You know how it is. And really, is it such a terrible thing to be a little bit sensitive?

[*He moves closer to Celia.*]

CELIA [*thrown*] It probably wasn't just that, though. It could have also been the way you dress. There was probably more she didn't like about you.... [*searching*] your B.O., your boring personality, maybe.

[*She looks off into space and flips her palms up as if at a loss. Slowly, she flips them inward and draws them together, indicating length.*]

CELIA Oh, I don't know....

LEWIS [*snapping up*] Probably all of it! That's the thing. We never did what you and I are doing now. We never sat and talked about it! If Laura would've been as open as you, I doubt things would've ended the way they did.

[*He smiles at her softly. She sits there, staring back, stunned into silence.*

The Director and Kenny APPROACH.]

DIRECTOR Celia?

[*Celia snaps out of it, CROSSES to them.*]

DIRECTOR Any progress?

CELIA Honestly? Lewis is the type who wouldn't kill a fly. Is there any chance we could just rewrite the scene?

KENNY The whole play revolves around that scene! I mean, you're making me rewrite this and that and I barely have time to sleep and....

DIRECTOR Pull it together, there, Ken. Jeez. [*to Celia*] Well, for the sake of your whole "Chekhov agenda," we're going to try this one more....

KENNY Come on, really, how difficult can it possibly be to want to kill your boss?!

DIRECTOR He's right, Celia. Get into character. Immerse yourself in the moment! [*announcing*] Top of the scene. Let's roll!

[*The Director, Kenny, and Lewis LEAVE THE SET. Celia sits at the desk and picks up the phone.*]

CELIA [*as YATES*] Uh huh. Yeah. I see. Yes, I'll need those figures by the end of the week.

[*As she talks, Lewis, as HENRY, APPROACHES from behind, wipes the sweat off his forehead.*]

DIRECTOR [*to LEWIS*] Whatever Henry's feeling, don't try to contain it! I want to see your blood boil, Lewis!

CELIA [*as YATES*] Yes, I understand, Bill. I do. It's a numbers game. You know that.

[*Lewis, as HENRY, looms eerily over Celia. He pulls the knife out of his pocket. His hand shakes.*]

DIRECTOR [*to LEWIS*] Don't hold anything back!

CELIA [*as YATES*] Yes. Yes, I'll call him in here. Hang on a minute. HENRY!

[*Celia swivels in her chair. Lewis, as HENRY, stares at her for a second. His knife CLANKS to the floor. He suddenly pulls her up for a KISS.*]

DIRECTOR [*exploding with rage*] What the hell is happening?!

[*Celia comes up for air.*]

CELIA [*swooning at Lewis*] You're the nicest guy I've ever met.

DIRECTOR I think I'm going to be sick. [*calling off*] Kenny!

[*Celia and Lewis embrace. The director CROSSES over to Kenny.*]

DIRECTOR It seems my actors are simply too. . . . lovable to perform your scene, so. . . .

[*As he continues, Kenny picks the knife up off the floor.*]

DIRECTOR . . . . I have no choice but to ask you rewrite it.

[*Knife in hand, Kenny steps closer to The Director.*]

DIRECTOR Though I really don't give a damn what you learned in drama school.

[*The knife shakes in Kenny's hand.*]

DIRECTOR It's a stupid principle, really, that just because there's a knife onstage, someone has to get stabbed. I'll need that rewrite by tomorrow, champ.

[*The Director playfully punches Kenny in the shoulder. In a moment of fury, Kenny feverishly STABS The Director in the chest. . . . But, since the knife is just a retractable stage prop, nothing happens. Kenny looks at the fake knife in horrified frustration. He THROWS it to the ground. The Director looks at him with surprise. After a moment. . . .*]

DIRECTOR You wouldn't happen to have any acting creds, would you?

As Kenny stares back miserably, THE LIGHTS. . . .

FADE TO BLACK

END OF PLAY

The Way Out

BY COLE HAMMACK

Copyright © by Cole Hammack. All rights reserved. Published with permission from the author. Inquiries concerning rights should be addressed to Cole Hammack at hammack.cole@gmail.com.

The Way Out

Premiered October 6, 2011 | Swain Hall, Studio 6 Theatre, UNC Department of Communication | Directed by Dana Coen

CHARACTERS

Original cast members are in brackets.

DANA 25, female. Works for the local unemployment office. [Haley Scruggs].

KATHY 40s, female. Recently suffered trauma [Christine Rogers].

DR. PHILLIPS 40s, male. An appointed therapist [Richard Jameyfield].

LINDA 20s, female. Kathy's daughter [Liz Phillips].

TOM 40s, male. Kathy's husband and Linda's father [Estes Tarver].

TIME & SETTING

Present. A suburban community, including various suggested locales: a park, Dana's apartment, a restaurant, Dr. Phillips's office, Kathy's living room.

SCENE ONE

LIGHTS UP

A DOOR upstage center SPLITS THE STAGE INTO TWO AREAS. Two women, ON OPPOSITE SIDES OF THE STAGE, sit, facing the audience.

AT STAGE LEFT, DANA sits in her apartment, fiddling with a SET OF KEYS.

AT STAGE RIGHT, KATHY sits on a park bench KNITTING A SWEATER.

After a few moments, THEIR CELL PHONES RING. They simultaneously pull them out. Kathy reads the screen on her phone, ignores the call, and places it back in her bag. Dana, anticipating her call, and despite her reluctance, ANSWERS.

DANA .... Hi.... My apartment.... Yeah, I know.... I was going to come.... I was.... Okay, okay.... Give me fifteen minutes.

[*Dana ENDS THE CALL, then slowly takes a deep breath.*]

[*KATHY'S phone RINGS again. Kathy pulls it out, checks the screen. This time she reluctantly answers. Kathy does not hide her emotions well.*]

KATHY What is it, honey?.... In the park.... Sitting.... Yeah.... Okay, but Linda.... just lunch.... That's fine.... I'll see you then.

[*Kathy ENDS THE CALL.*]

END OF SCENE

SCENE TWO

STAGE RIGHT, Kathy sits in the waiting area of a restaurant, staring at a menu.

STAGE LEFT, Dana sits in silence with DR. PHILLIPS, a therapist. She continues to fiddle with the keys.

DR. PHILLIPS We don't have to talk about it.

DANA Good.

DR. PHILLIPS Anything else you want to discuss?

DANA Nope.

DR. PHILLIPS Is there something you want to ask me?

DANA Yeah, can I smoke in here?

DR. PHILLIPS No.

DANA Really?

DR. PHILLIPS Really.

DANA It's okay, I don't smoke.

[*Dana returns to silence.*]

[*STAGE RIGHT, Kathy's daughter LINDA APPEARS and sits next to Kathy.*]

LINDA It's a twenty-minute wait, is that okay?

KATHY Uh, huh.

LINDA [*opening her menu*] What are you getting?

KATHY Don't know. Nothing on here looks good.

LINDA You're reading the wine list.

KATHY Yeah.

LINDA The Brie and apple sandwich is amazing.

KATHY I'll probably get the club, on wheat.

LINDA [*trying to lighten the mood*] Oh come on, Mom. That's so boring! Try the Brie.

KATHY I want the club.

LINDA Order the Brie. If you don't like it, we can get the club.

[*Silence from Kathy. The argument is over.*]

LINDA Okay, you can have a bite of mine. You are so stubborn. [*continued silence*] Ever been here?

KATHY No, too far from home.

LINDA [*carefully testing the waters*] I can change that.

KATHY Linda, I don't want to talk about the house.

[*STAGE LEFT, Dana turns to Dr. Phillips.*]

DANA Okay, I have a question.

DR. PHILLIPS Go ahead.

DANA What's your name?

DR. PHILLIPS Dr. Phillips.

DANA Your full name.

DR. PHILLIPS Ronald Delaware Phillips.

DANA [*mocking*] Are you serious?

DR. PHILLIPS Yes.

DANA Are you from Delaware?

DR. PHILLIPS No, Michigan.

DANA Where did you go to college?

DR. PHILLIPS Michigan for undergrad, and I have my law degree from Penn.

DANA Are you married?

DR. PHILLIPS No.

DANA Girlfriend?

DR. PHILLIPS No.

DANA Really?

DR. PHILLIPS I had a fiancée at one time.

DANA What happened?

DR. PHILLIPS She asked too many questions.

[*A slight smile from Dana. She's been trumped.*]

[*STAGE RIGHT, Kathy and Linda. Kathy is now knitting her sweater.*]

LINDA I've been running lately. John and I signed up for a half-marathon in May. Want to join us?

KATHY No thanks.

LINDA You used to run. [*beat*] It's not good to just sit and knit.

KATHY It's easier than a half-marathon.

LINDA You need an activity. This has been hard for me too, but with something to focus on, it's. . . .

KATHY [*finishing her sentence*] . . . . your prerogative.

LINDA [*coming out with it*] Let me help you sell the house. You can't afford it, and I don't like thinking of you sitting alone in that place. We should have never moved there to begin with. . . . too big, too expensive. We need to put it behind us.

KATHY What you mean to say, is that I need to put *him* behind me?

LINDA No, I. . . .

KATHY You can choose to ignore your father, but I will not. [*aggressively*] I knew him first!

[*Kathy returns to her knitting.*]

[*STAGE LEFT, Dr. Phillips and Dana*]

DR. PHILLIPS [*re: the keys*] You always do that?

DANA What?

DR. PHILLIPS Play with your keys?

[*Dana chooses not to answer.*]

DR. PHILLIPS A lot is represented there. . . . house, car, most of one's worldly possessions.

[*STAGE RIGHT, Linda and Kathy*]

LINDA I asked a realtor to make up a flyer.

[*Linda pulls a flyer out of her purse, hands it to Kathy.*]

LINDA Just look at it.

[*Kathy accepts it, skims it.*]

[*STAGE LEFT, Dana and Dr. Phillips*]

DR. PHILLIPS [*re: the keys*] Do they mean something to you?

DANA Now *you're* asking too many questions.

[*STAGE RIGHT, Linda and Kathy*]

LINDA I think the price is fair, given what happened.

KATHY Have you not heard a thing I've said?

LINDA I'm....

KATHY [*upset*] I can't talk to you!

[*STAGE LEFT, Dana and Dr. Phillips*]

DR. PHILLIPS [*re: the keys*] Then, maybe you should put them away.

DANA I can't do that either.

[*Both Kathy and Dana RISE.*]

LINDA & **DR. PHILLIPS** [*simultaneously*] Where are you going?

KATHY & **DANA** [*simultaneously*] Home.

DR. PHILLIPS [*to Dana*] Really?

DANA No....

END OF SCENE

SCENE THREE

AT MID-STAGE, Kathy and Dana are standing in Kathy's living room.

DANA [*looking around*] It's a lovely house.

KATHY Thank you. [*pause*] Do I need to sign something? I wasn't really listening on the phone.

DANA No, nothing like that.

KATHY Good, all the bureaucratic stuff from the unemployment office confuses me. Please sit.

[*Both sit. Kathy begins knitting her sweater.*]

KATHY So, how can I help you?

[*Dana focuses on the wall behind Kathy.*]

DANA That your daughter?

KATHY Excuse me?

DANA The painting on the wall.

KATHY Yes.

DANA Any other children?

KATHY No, just her.

DANA So, she grew up here?

KATHY We got the house when she was sixteen. She never liked it. But my husband's business was doing well, and the market was hot, and.... I'm sorry, why are you here again?

DANA Oh, I.... [*suddenly struck*] I wanted to....

[*Dana reaches into her pocket, then quickly changes her mind.*]

DANA You know what? I better go. [*Dana RISES.*]

KATHY I don't understand.

DANA My apologies. I made a mistake.

KATHY What do you mean?

DANA [*almost to herself*] I should have been nicer to him.

[*Kathy blocks her way.*]

KATHY Who are you?

[*Dana tries to move past her.*]

KATHY I'll call the police!

[*Dana stops.*]

KATHY [*beat, realization*] Were you the girl who was with him?

[*Beat. Dana nods.*]

KATHY Please, don't go.

[*Dana eyes the door.*]

KATHY Really. I insist.

[*Slowly, they both RETURN to their chairs.*]

KATHY Tea?

DANA No.

KATHY [*beat*] I'm waiting.

DANA [*beat, then . . .*] I was sitting at my desk when he walked in.

[*TOM ENTERS through the CENTER DOORWAY and STANDS UPSTAGE BETWEEN KATHY AND DANA.*]

DANA He was fidgeting with my stapler. I told him to put it down.

TOM [*to Dana*] I'm sorry.

DANA [*to Kathy*] I asked him his name.

TOM [*to Dana*] Thomas Braxton Parker.

DANA [*to Kathy*] He gave me the forms, told me he needed an extension. He said he didn't have a job and that he was behind on his house payments. So I asked him if he had been looking.

KATHY [*answering, to Dana*] Every day.

TOM [*to Dana*] Just no one is hiring at my level. I've had some odd jobs but nothing permanent.

DANA [*to Kathy*] I told him I was going to have to deny him another extension.

TOM [*to Dana*] I just need a few more months.

DANA [*to Kathy*] I had no say in the matter.

TOM [*to Dana*] Is there someone at the main office I can call?

DANA [*to Kathy*] But, I could have been nicer.

[*Tom reaches for his cell phone, but pulls out a HANDGUN. Kathy STIFFENS at the revelation.*]

TOM [*to Dana*] Oh. Sorry. Bet you didn't expect that, huh? Forgot I had it.

DANA [*to Kathy*] I couldn't speak.

TOM [*to Dana*] Bought it at a pawn shop, cost twenty bucks. My house had been burglarized.

DANA [*to Kathy*] He started rambling about all kinds of things.

TOM [*to Dana*] You know, you think you're safe, but really. . . .

DANA [*to Kathy*] They seemed unrelated.

TOM [*to Dana*] My brother complains of indigestion one day, is dead the next.

DANA [*to Kathy*] I didn't hear much of it. . . . except for your name.

TOM [*to Dana*] Kathy loves the house. It's everything her parents couldn't. . . .

DANA [*to Kathy*] He kept bringing it up and how he had disappointed you.

KATHY [*to Dana*] I thought he was having an affair.

TOM [*turning to Kathy*] What? No, that's crazy.

KATHY [*to Dana*] I was searching through his closet for evidence, and I found the gun in one of his boots.

TOM [*to Kathy*] It's for safety, protection!

KATHY [*to Dana*] I couldn't believe he brought it into our home. I ordered him to take it with him.

TOM [*to Kathy*] Where?

KATHY [*to Dana*] I pushed it into his chest. So, he put it in his pocket.

TOM [*to Kathy*] Fine.

KATHY [*long beat, to Dana*] And then he left. . . .

[*Very slowly and deliberately, Tom brings the muzzle of the gun up and under his chin and FREEZES.*]

KATHY . . . . us. [*long beat*] Why did you come here?

[*Dana slowly pulls out the keys from her pocket, offers them to Kathy, who GASPS with grief.*]

DANA I found them under my desk after the police left. Your address is on the metal tag.

KATHY His door key never worked very well. He would stand there for minutes, fiddling with it. I would hear it and let him in.

[*A long moment of silence as both women deeply share what has been, up to this point, a very private grieving process. Shortly, Dana points to Kathy's knitting.*]

DANA Was that for him?

[*Kathy nods.*]

DANA I'm so sorry.

KATHY That makes two of us.

[*Kathy RISES.*]

KATHY Let me walk you out.

[*Dana RISES. As they cross upstage, they pass Tom on either side, and EXIT through the door. Kathy CLOSES it behind them.*]

[*Tom lowers the gun to his side.*]

[*After a beat, both women now RETURN to their original places on OPPOSITE SIDES OF THE STAGE. Dana, back in her apartment, SITS and reveals the SWEATER Kathy was knitting. She now begins to knit it herself.*]

[*Kathy, now FIDDLING WITH THE KEYS, returns to the park bench. She inspects them for a long moment, then pulls out her cell phone and dials.*]

KATHY Hi honey.... In the park. [*beat*] I'm sorry about yesterday.

[*Kathy takes out the crinkled house flyer Linda had given her and scans it for a moment.*]

KATHY So, about this price. [*beat*] Let's lower it.

[*As she listens to her daughter's response, THE LIGHTS....*]

FADE TO BLACK

END OF PLAY

Seasoning

BY XINGYUE SARAH HE

Copyright © by Xingyue Sarah He. All rights reserved. Published with permission from the author. Inquiries concerning rights should be addressed to Xingyue Sarah He at xingyueshe3715@gmail.com.

Seasoning

Presented October 23, 2015 | Kenan Theatre, UNC Department of Dramatic Art | Directed by Serena Ebhardt

CHARACTERS

Original cast members are in brackets.

SANYA KONG 20s, Chinese female. Recently married to Maddock; has a Ph.D., but can't find a job [Mackenzie Kwok].

MADDOCK GEORGE 20s, East Indian male. Married to Sanya and in the process of getting his Ph.D. in biomedical engineering [Jerome Allen].

GREG OWENS 50s, male. Sanya and Maddock's neighbor from two doors down [Bill Garrity].

TIME & SETTING

Present. Sanya and Maddock's apartment in New York City.

SCENE ONE

LIGHTS UP

On MADDOCK GEORGE as he STRUGGLES to put a crooked, artificial Christmas tree up on its chipped stand. On the tree hang plastic Sears ornaments. SANYA KONG pushes away and flattens a stray tree branch that is poking Maddock in the cheek.

> **SANYA** [*with a Chinese accent*] Aren't you glad you came shopping with me this morning, instead of working in the lab?

MADDOCK [*with an Indian accent*] I'm going to have to catch up next week.

SANYA [*rolling her eyes jokingly*] Yeah, yeah. You have a world to save.

[*Maddock secures the tree in the stand.*]

MADDOCK But this was a good find. Just don't tell anyone we got it at Sears.

SANYA You mean from the *dumpsters* behind Sears.

MADDOCK [*fake concern*] Shhh! Someone can hear you!

SANYA We're just using it so it doesn't go to waste.

MADDOCK No one back at home would waste such a perfectly good tree. Even if it is fake.

SANYA Well, we're in America now.

[*She plays with the mismatched plastic Sears ornaments as Maddock tries to straighten the crooked tree trunk.*]

MADDOCK How does it look?

SANYA Great.

MADDOCK I can't straighten it.

SANYA It's fine. It won't be too long before we'll have a real tree.

[*Maddock removes the ornaments from the tree. Sanya strokes the branches as if it were a pet.*]

SANYA By then you'll have finished your doctorate and I'll have finally gotten a job. We can even get a wreath and gifts with ribbons, wrapped all up in shiny paper, and have a feast too. . . . with a turkey!

MADDOCK I think that's Thanksgiving.

SANYA Oh, I thought they ate turkey for everything. . . . except for the Fourth of July. Then they eat hot dogs.

MADDOCK Here, help me.

[*Together, they strain to straighten the tree. It doesn't budge.*]

MADDOCK I think they eat ham at Christmas. Maybe.

SANYA Ham, turkey, whatever. We'll learn it all eventually, and then we'll be like everyone else. We'll be Americans.

MADDOCK If you say so. Let's try bending it the other way.

[*They make another attempt. The tree straightens a bit, but not fully.*]

[*There is a KNOCK AT THE DOOR.*]

[*Maddock CROSSES TO THE DOOR and peers through the peephole.*]

SANYA [*concerned*] Sears people?

MADDOCK No, just Greg.

SANYA From two doors down?

MADDOCK Should I open it?

SANYA Sure, let him in.

[*Maddock opens the door, revealing GREG OWENS in a red-felt padded Santa suit, lopsided red hat, and a white strap-on beard. He holds a LUMPY RED BAG in his hand.*]

GREG Hey guys.

SANYA Come in, Greg. Have a seat.

[*Greg stumbles in, a little unsteady, a little drunk. Sanya gives the couch a fluff. Greg drops his bag but doesn't sit.*]

MADDOCK Just get off work?

GREG An hour ago.

[*Greg wanders around the apartment, approaches the desk.*]

SANYA So Greg, why have you come to see us?

[*Greg pauses by a COIN COLLECTION displayed in a cardboard stand.*]

GREG Is this new?

MADDOCK No, we just didn't unpack it until recently.

GREG They worth anything?

MADDOCK Yeah, these Seated Liberty Half Dollars are worth about fifty-something each.

[*Greg takes a coin out of the stand and flips it around in his hands.*]

GREG [*impressed*] Whoa!

[*He accidently drops it on the floor. Maddock picks it up and carefully puts it back on the stand. The three of them stand in awkward silence.*]

SANYA Can I get you something to drink?

GREG Yeah, you got beer?

SANYA How about tea? I already have some steeped.

[*Sanya EXITS.*]

MADDOCK Getting a lot of that holiday spirit at work?

GREG No, not at all. The kids are annoying and ask questions that I don't have the answers to. You know, like why do you live at the North Pole and not the South, or what kind of engine my sleigh runs on.

[*Sanya ENTERS with a cup of tea.*]

MADDOCK Wow, those are smart kids.

[*Sanya hands Greg the cup of tea. He just sets it down on a table.*]

GREG The worst is when the adults want to sit on your lap and take twenty pictures.

[*Another uncomfortable pause.*]

SANYA Have you been home yet, Greg?

GREG Yeah.

[*He slumps down on the couch and sighs.*]

GREG But Cynthia tossed all my things out onto the staircase and locked me out.

SANYA I'm sorry.

[*Greg grabs his bag and starts pulling things out. . . . a plastic train, a few books. . . .*]

GREG I just had a few beers. It wasn't even that much.

[*He continues to unload his bag, which includes a fake gun and a stuffed bear. Some of his dirty clothes and socks fall out of the bag along with the toys.*]

SANYA [*concerned*] Why do you have a gun?

[*Greg picks up the gun.*]

GREG It's just a toy. My boy loves to play with them. These were all for him. [*upset*] I wasn't going to hit anyone this time. I really wasn't! I mean, I fucking stole these from the store!

[*He takes off his beard and hat and buries his head in his hands. Silence. Now what?*]

SANYA Would you like me to talk with Cynthia?

GREG No, no. Just go back to whatever you're doing. Is it okay if I just sit here for a bit?

SANYA Oh, sure, of course.

MADDOCK Take your time.

SANYA We're just setting up our tree.

[*Maddock and Sanya take inventory of the ornaments.*]

MADDOCK I think if we put the blue ones on this side, and the red and silver ones across. . . .

SANYA I think it would look better if we just interchange them a little.

MADDOCK But there are not enough blues.

SANYA Greg, what do you think?

[*Greg looks up, lost.*]

GREG What?

SANYA How do you think we should place these ornaments? None of them match.

GREG Just pretend they're all the same and throw them on.

[*Greg RISES and haphazardly throws some of the ornaments on the tree.*]

SANYA [*trying to make the best of it*] That looks good.

MADDOCK [*to Greg*] Good thing you were here.

[*Greg begins to stuff the toys back into his red bag.*]

GREG Well, I guess I should be going.

MADDOCK Where will you go?

GREG I don't know. Somewhere.

SANYA [*checking with Maddock*] Why don't you just stay here tonight?

MADDOCK Yeah, we don't mind. If you don't mind the couch.

GREG Oh no, I shouldn't.

MADDOCK Please, be our guest.

SANYA You can help us, like you did with the tree.

[*Greg stops packing.*]

GREG Alright, okay.

SANYA I'll get you a blanket and pillow. And Maddock can find something for you to wear for the night.

MADDOCK We'll be right back. Try the tea. Sanya brought it over from China.

[*Sanya and Maddock EXIT. Greg sniffs the tea. The sniff turns into a SOB. He CRIES quietly.*]

END OF SCENE

SCENE TWO

Sanya ENTERS in her pajamas, still shaking off the night's sleep. On the couch, a folded blanket and pillow remain untouched. The toy gun lies on the ground by the couch.

SANYA Would you like some eggs and toast? [*She rubs her eyes and realizes no one is in the living room.*] Greg?

[*Maddock ENTERS.*]

SANYA Where did he go?

MADDOCK I guess he took off.

[*She picks up the blanket and pillow from the couch.*]

SANYA Maybe Cynthia will take him back. Poor man.

MADDOCK Maybe she will. He's not a bad guy.

[*Sanya notices the toy gun on the floor. She hands the blanket and pillow to Maddock.*]

SANYA Here, take these. He dropped one of his toys.

[*She picks up the toy gun and sets it on the table.*]

SANYA [*surprised*] Oh. Where did your silver half-dollars go?

MADDOCK What do you mean? They're on the table.

SANYA No they're not.

[*Maddock drops the pillow and blanket and rushes over.*]

MADDOCK [*slow realization*] He took my coin collection!

SANYA Greg? But why?

MADDOCK We let him stay here! We.... [*turning to Sanya*] *You* let him.

SANYA What? I let him? You opened the door!

MADDOCK Only after I asked *you*.

SANYA Well, we couldn't just let him be homeless! He was Santa Claus!

MADDOCK What are we going to do? That was my backup plan!

SANYA What?

MADDOCK I was going to sell those coins. They're worth a lot more together.... a small fortune!

[*He picks up the gun from the table and throws it at the couch.*]

SANYA Well, you'll get a job when you're done.

MADDOCK What if I don't?

SANYA I'll get a job.

MADDOCK You haven't been able to yet!

SANYA We'll figure out a way. We have to. We've got rent and loans....

MADDOCK I'm calling 911.

[*Pulling out his cell phone, Maddock dials, waits. Sanya picks up the toy gun from the couch, inspects it.*]

MADDOCK Yes. I would like to report a robbery. His name is Greg Owens.

SANYA I will have to try again. I have a Ph.D., after all.

MADDOCK [*on the phone*] Edward Skull Village, apartment 8H. [*to Sanya*] They put me on hold.

SANYA Or I'll go mop floors at McDonald's.

MADDOCK [*into phone*] Hello?

SANYA That's the American way.

[*Sanya CROSSES to the tree and HANGS THE TOY GUN from one of its crooked branches.*]

MADDOCK [*into phone*] Hello? I'm still here.

[*As Maddock continues to wait, Sanya quietly but determinedly HUMS the Christmas carol "Deck the Halls."*]

FADE TO BLACK

END OF PLAY

A Failuretale

BY ELIZABETH HYLTON

Copyright © by Elizabeth Hylton. All rights reserved. Published with permission from the author. Inquiries concerning rights should be addressed to Elizabeth Hylton at elizabethfriday@gmail.com.

A Failuretale

Presented October 3, 2014 | Swain Hall, Studio 6 Theatre, UNC Department of Communication | Directed by Serena Ebhardt

CHARACTERS
Original cast members are in brackets.

ARIEL 20, female, with long red hair [Maggie Poole].

AURORA 20, female, with blond hair [Camille Oswald].

RAPUNZEL 20, female, with very long blond hair [Nicola Bullock].

TIME & SETTING
Present. The women's restroom at a party site.

SCENE ONE

LIGHTS UP

On a women's restroom. UPBEAT MUSIC from the PARTY outside is heard. Three sinks stand in a row downstage. On a platform behind the sinks are three bathroom stalls. We can see TWO HEELED FEET underneath the middle stall. ARIEL and AURORA ENTER.

ARIEL I just think it's ridiculous how everyone comes to these things and ends up hooking up with each other. I mean, come on. I know I'm lucky. I have a husband. But for God's sake, people. I'm just here to have fun, not get an STD.

AURORA Yeah. Totally.

ARIEL Sometimes I feel way too old for this. Am I being judgy? Do you know what I mean?

AURORA Uh huh.

[*Aurora and Ariel, facing the audience, touch up their makeup and smooth their hair in what we imagine are mirrors over the sinks.*]

ARIEL Okay, okay. Jasmine last weekend. I was embarrassed for her. Jasmine, we get it, you're hot, you're sexy, you're lonely, you have daddy issues. But three guys in one night?

AURORA [*hazy*] Oh. . . . yeah. . . .

ARIEL Right. I forgot you were totally out that night. . . . on that stuff.

AURORA . . . . For my headaches.

ARIEL You need more sleep, Aurora.

[*A toilet FLUSHES. The middle stall door opens and out steps RAPUNZEL. She CROSSES to the middle sink and begins to wash her hands. Both Ariel and Aurora stare. A moment passes.*]

ARIEL [*almost resentfully*] I like your hair.

RAPUNZEL Thanks.

[*Ariel reaches out as if about to touch it. Rapunzel steps back abruptly to avoid her hand.*]

RAPUNZEL Don't.

ARIEL Oh wow. I didn't. . . .

RAPUNZEL [*simultaneously*] I'm a little. . . . weird. . . . about my hair.

ARIEL Sorry.

[*There's an awkward silence.*]

ARIEL [*realization*] Wait. Holy shit. Rapunzel?

RAPUNZEL Ariel?

[*The two SQUEAL and embrace.*]

RAPUNZEL Please tell me everything you have been up to.

ARIEL Well, you know.... getting.... married! Four years this spring!

[*Ariel whips out her ringed left hand. More SQUEALS.*]

RAPUNZEL That is a dream. Is he here?

ARIEL Eric? Yes! I can't wait for you to meet him. Are you dating anyone?

RAPUNZEL Kind-of-not-really. As of today actually. I was.... but I felt a little tied down so.... we decided to redefine things.

ARIEL Wow, I'm so sorry.

RAPUNZEL No, no, actually it's.... Thanks.

[*Another uncomfortable pause. The MUSIC outside the bathroom CHANGES. Aurora begins to HUM along with the tune.*]

ARIEL Oh my God, I'm so rude. This is my friend Aurora.

RAPUNZEL [*to Aurora*] I love your shoes.

AURORA Thank you.

[*The conversation dies. Aurora continues to hum along to the music. Ariel begins to SING along. RAPUNZEL JOINS IN. Ariel gets a little LOUDER. In response, Aurora starts to HARMONIZE. Ariel sings EVEN LOUDER. It's getting awkward.*]

RAPUNZEL [*to Ariel*] I'm so glad I ran into you two. This is going to be great.

ARIEL Yes. I've been needing this. And guess what I brought...?

[*Ariel reveals a flask that had been hidden in her dress.*]

ARIEL Cheers!

RAPUNZEL With the fun flask, what could go wrong? I have a good feeling about tonight.

[*The ladies link arms and head offstage. The PARTY MUSIC SWELLS.*]

END OF SCENE

SCENE TWO

Again, TWO FEET are clearly visible underneath one of the stall doors. We hear MUSIC from the PARTY OUTSIDE.

Ariel and Rapunzel ENTER, stumbling and giggly.

ARIEL Where did you disappear off to earlier?

RAPUNZEL Oh you know, just exploring. . . .

ARIEL You're so bad. I'm totally starting to feel it. Let's text someone.

RAPUNZEL Who?

ARIEL I don't know . . . . Eric! Let's text him we're making out in here!

[*They both erupt into LAUGHTER. Ariel types out a message and sends it.*]

RAPUNZEL I want to see his face when he gets it.

[*They OPEN THE DOOR SLIGHTLY and PEEK OUT into the party.*]

ARIEL Aw, look at him. He's so jealous. [*pause*] Oh my God. . . . !

RAPUNZEL What?

ARIEL Jasmine. Going at it with. . . .

RAPUNZEL Didn't she and Aladdin just break up? And she's already *hooking* up?

ARIEL I know, right? And not with just anyone.

RAPUNZEL Wait. . . . is that. . . . ?

ARIEL Philip.

RAPUNZEL Philip Philip? Aurora's Philip? [*beat*] Oh no.

ARIEL I told you I thought he was cheating, didn't I? And it's not like he's even trying to hide it.

RAPUNZEL [*guilty*] Hey Ariel, remember when I said I was exploring . . . ?

ARIEL [*realization*] You didn't.

RAPUNZEL [*beat*] I did.

ARIEL Damn.

RAPUNZEL I didn't know it was Philip Philip!

ARIEL Whatever. It's Jasmine with her tongue down his throat now.

RAPUNZEL Oh God! I should tell Aurora.

ARIEL I'm sure she knows. This isn't, let's just say, the first time for Philip.

RAPUNZEL That's so effed up. And she doesn't do anything?

ARIEL The girl has no self-respect.

RAPUNZEL She is a bit of a wet blanket.

ARIEL To say the least. She is so naive sometimes. A pretty face and an okay singer, but clearly her godmothers did not think to bless her with intelligence when she was born. Or even personality. That's got to get old pretty fast. I mean, come on, I hate to be the one to say it, but can you blame him?

[*The STALL DOOR OPENS abruptly to reveal Aurora.*]

[*Stunned silence. Aurora slowly CROSSES to a sink and begins to wash her hands.*]

AURORA [*an attempt at dignity*] Ariel, could you pass me that hand towel?

[*Ariel passes her the towel.*]

RAPUNZEL Listen, Aurora, I didn't know it was. . . . those things we said about you and Philip. . . . you know what, that was really out of line. We're just jealous because you're so pretty and such a good singer.

ARIEL No. That's not even true.

RAPUNZEL Well yes, you are really pretty and a really good singer.

ARIEL Aurora, open your eyes. This is getting pathetic.

RAPUNZEL [*simultaneously*] What Ariel means is. . . .

ARIEL As your friend. . . .

RAPUNZEL Yes! Friends!

ARIEL I can't let this go on any longer. You need to get your shit together and stand up for yourself. Grow up and try having an adult relationship.

AURORA An adult relationship?

ARIEL Yeah, an adult relationship.

RAPUNZEL I think we all are pretty mature in our relationships.

AURORA Please, Ariel. Spare me the marriage lecture.

ARIEL You are so condescending. For once, just accept I know more about healthy relationships than you.

AURORA You dated for three days when you were sixteen and then you got married. So healthy.

RAPUNZEL [*to Ariel*] Wow. Really? That's what happened?

ARIEL You met Philip once in the woods and decided it was love at first sight. That sounds pretty fucking creepy to me.

RAPUNZEL Okay, that is a little creepy.

AURORA [*lashing out at Rapunzel*] What does this have to do with you? Why are you here?

RAPUNZEL First of all, FYI, I didn't know it was Philip Philip. He seemed nice, by the way. Second of all, I'm in an open relationship. I recommend it for you.

AURORA Aw, sweetie. You must be kidding yourself.

RAPUNZEL What? Two mature adults should be able to have an understanding and enjoy themselves without all the drama of labels.

AURORA Sounds like he gets his cake and eats it, too.

RAPUNZEL Yeah, well I had your cake and it wasn't even that good.

AURORA [*looking Rapunzel up and down*] Maybe you should think about cutting back on the desserts.

RAPUNZEL Excuse me? Are you calling me fat?

AURORA And a slut.

RAPUNZEL It's not my fault your boyfriend cheats on you.

AURORA At least I actually have a boyfriend.

ARIEL See, it's unnecessary drama like this that's eliminated when you have fully committed your life to someone.

[*Ariel's phone BUZZES. She checks.*]

ARIEL Excuse me. My husband is calling.

[*Ariel ANSWERS her phone as Aurora and Rapunzel glare at each other.*]

ARIEL [*into phone*] Hey, babe. . . . no, I'm in the bathroom. . . . what? No, hon, that was a joke. . . . .It was a joke!. . . . Only a few, but that's not the point. . . . God, would you just listen to me?! Babe, would you just take a fucking joke. . . . Just listen!. . . . Will you ever lis. . . . Yeah? Well you go right ahead and go. . . . see if I care!

[*Ariel ENDS THE CALL, takes a moment. . . . and begins to CRY. Aurora and Rapunzel shift into empathy mode.*]

ARIEL He says he's leaving.

RAPUNZEL Well, who needs him to have fun, anyway?

AURORA It's not like he would *actually* leave you.

ARIEL That's true.

RAPUNZEL We don't even need them.

AURORA Yeah.

[*The three women go in for a group hug. Aurora stops, catching a scent of Rapunzel. She staggers backward.*]

AURORA God, I can smell him all over you!!!

[*Liked a wounded animal, Aurora retreats to the middle stall and slams the door.*]

ARIEL Now look what you did.

[*Rapunzel CROSSES up to the stall.*]

RAPUNZEL [*through the stall door*] Aurora, listen to me, I'm sorry. It didn't mean anything. I didn't know it was him. But, Aurora. . . . are you listening to me? You should stop letting him do this to you. Come on.

[*Ariel's phone BUZZES. She's so excited she drops it, dives to get it, and finally manages to answer.*]

ARIEL [*into phone*] Eric?.... Wait, Dad? Why are you calling me? I'm busy. Leave me alone.

RAPUNZEL I'm going to find Philip.

[*She EXITS.*]

ARIEL [*into phone, breaking down*] Daddy, I'm having a hard time. I.... I try to make him happy. I do the bit with the fork, but he doesn't think it's cute anymore. And he used to ask me to sing. Now any time I do, he turns up the music really loud.

[*Rapunzel RE-ENTERS with a kitchen knife.*]

ARIEL [*into phone*] Dad, I have to go.

[*Ariel ENDS THE CALL.*]

RAPUNZEL You know what would make us feel better?

[*Rapunzel turns to the mirror and begins shearing off her own hair in stabbing hacks.*]

ARIEL Did you see Eric?

RAPUNZEL A change. That's what would make us feel better. Eric and Philip left. But we don't need them.

[*Ariel watches for a moment, then makes a CALL.*]

ARIEL [*into the phone, over voice mail*] Hey, babe. It's me. Just wondering what you were up to. I'm in the bathroom. Could you give me a call back when you get the chance? Love you!

[*Rapunzel finishes. HER HAIR IS NOW SHORT.*]

RAPUNZEL I feel much better. You should try this. Aurora! Come try it. It's freeing. BE FREE!

[*Rapunzel DROPS THE KNIFE on the floor, CROSSES to Aurora's stall door, and pulls at the handle. It's LOCKED. After a few moments, she gives up. Aurora crawls out from under the stall door, as if swimming.*]

RAPUNZEL Aurora?

[*Aurora RISES and looks around. She COOS softly and SWATS HER HANDS at the air in front of her. After a moment, she begins an elaborately choreographed DANCE, like she's under water, moving her limbs slowly and deliberately. She stops and speaks directly at Ariel.*]

AURORA Hey, look.

[*She PASSES OUT, falls to the floor. Rapunzel runs to her, then checks out her stall.*]

RAPUNZEL What the fuck did she take?

ARIEL Her medicine. It's to help her sleep.

[*Rapunzel reveals a SYRINGE.*]

RAPUNZEL You're kidding me, right?

[*Rapunzel CROSSES back to Aurora, who is conscious but in a dreamlike state. GUIDING HER BACK INTO THE STALL, she props Aurora on the ground in front of the toilet. Ariel begins to WEEP loudly. From her stall, Aurora begins to SING NONSENSE WORDS. Ariel picks up the discarded kitchen knife from the floor and MAKES ANOTHER PHONE CALL.*]

ARIEL [*into her phone, desperately cheerful*] Hey, you! It's Ariel. I think you might have lost your phone.

[*Ariel begins to REPEATEDLY STAB THE KNIFE INTO THE FLOOR.*]

ARIEL Well, I'm here in the bathroom when you get this. So. . . . come when you get this! Anyway, I love you, babe.

[*Rapunzel leaves Aurora slumped in the stall, CROSSES to Ariel, and pries the knife from her hand. She then gazes at both Ariel and Aurora for a long moment.*]

RAPUNZEL It'll be okay. I have a good feeling about tonight.

[*She sets the knife on the edge of the middle sink and EXITS. Aurora begins to SING again.*]

FADE TO BLACK

END OF PLAY

Snowmen

BY CHARLIE KELSEY

Copyright © by Charlie Kelsey. All rights reserved. Published with permission from the author. Inquiries concerning rights should be addressed to Charlie Kelsey at charliekelsey12@gmail.com.

Snowmen

Presented October 23, 2015 | Kenan Theatre, UNC Department of Dramatic Art | Directed by David Henderson

CHARACTERS

Original cast members are in brackets.

CRAWFORD TYNE 36, male. A former mercenary in Somalia [Mark Jantzen].

ALAN TYNE 32, male, Crawford's younger brother. A mercenary, recently returned from Somalia [Brook North].

LEYENNE TYNE 36, female, Crawford's wife [A. C. Donohue].

HEN TYNE 29, female, Alan's wife [Claire Koenig].

TIME & SETTING

Present. A suburban home in a Midwestern city.

LIGHTS UP

On a comfortable living room, with expertly hung CHRISTMAS DECORATIONS. CHEERY CHRISTMAS MUSIC plays from a TINNY RADIO. A fire crackles in the grate, and a warm light radiates throughout the room. Outside, the snow falls slowly and heavily. CRAWFORD TYNE is seated on a couch, flipping through a photo album. ALAN TYNE stands at the window, finishing up his drink, and staring out at the snow.

CRAWFORD Shit, man. Look at this.

[*He holds up a photo to Alan, who turns around to look at it.*]

ALAN [*smiles sadly*] I'm a fucking mess in that one. What was it, ten stitches to the dome? Christmas Eve in the ER?

CRAWFORD Woulda been a lot worse if I wasn't there, thank Christ.

ALAN Thank Christ the motherfucker wasn't too drunk to swerve.

[*LEYENNE TYNE saunters into the room, clutching several beers. HEN TYNE FOLLOWS quietly behind her.*]

LEYENNE Enough nostalgia for one day. The little bastard's tucked up in your bed. [*chuckling*] It's about twenty times his size. Mama needs to drink.

[*Leyenne perches herself on the arm of the couch beside Crawford. Hen quietly sinks into an armchair.*]

LEYENNE Only beer, but I thought we might want to consider easing into the swing. [*beat*] It's been a long time since we had a boozy family Christmas in this house.

CRAWFORD [*kisses Leyenne*] Been a long time since we were all together, darling.

LEYENNE I'm just glad to have our heroes back. Did Crawford tell you the news yet, Alan?

[*As Alan turns to her and CROSSES over, he drags his right leg behind him as if it's heavier than the other. He sinks into the couch.*]

ALAN What news?

CRAWFORD [*nervously*] I think we're trying for another kid.

LEYENNE My husband is hopeless. We *are* trying for another kid. We want to give you a niece. Merry Christmas!

[*Alan finishes his drink with a long swig and forces a smile.*]

ALAN That's fantastic. Congratulations.... [*beat*] .... to both of you.

LEYENNE Don't toss around any commendations until the kid graduates high school with all its arms and legs. [*pause*] And might our gruesome twosome have a cousin, Hen? [*carefully*] It really can be a phenomenal experience for a family. . . .

ALAN [*coldly*] Not really the right time, Leyenne.

[*CRACK. The SOUND OF A BRANCH SNAPPING can be heard from outside.*]

ALAN [*startled*] What the fuck was that?

CRAWFORD It's a branch or something.

LEYENNE [*laughs*] You've been gone too long. When you spend a couple of holiday seasons in a big house, all alone. . . . you realize the world can be a noisy place in the winter. Hen knows.

HEN [*quietly*] At least you had Crawford for the last one.

[*It's the first time she's spoken, and it cuts through the room like a knife. Crawford and Alan fall silent.*]

LEYENNE [*picking up the conversation*] Maybe some darker waters? [*pauses*] Vino Rojo for the bolder soul, perhaps?

CRAWFORD That's a great idea. Hen?

HEN [*quietly*] I should start dinner. [*beat*] Maybe we should wait before we start pouring again.

LEYENNE It's the holiday.

[*Leyenne stands up and uncorks some wine. She pours three glasses. She holds one out to Hen. Alan, having put down his empty glass, grabs it instead, and takes a long swig. Leyenne looks at her husband, uneasy, but nobody says anything.*]

ALAN You know what's fucked up, Craw? [*a long pause*] It's Christmas. And I can't even do my favorite thing. I can't even build a goddamn snowman.

CRAWFORD   That one we made when I was nine. . . . terrifying.

ALAN   [*smiles*] Gave Mom nightmares.

[*Crawford attempts to take the glass from Alan. Alan ignores him. No chance.*]

LEYENNE   [*to Crawford, a warning*] Let's not, sweetheart.

[*Leyenne stares Crawford down. He's powerless. He sits back down, beaten.*]

ALAN   [*chuckles*] Don't let the prison warden catch you out of bed after hours, brother. [*ignoring Leyenne*] She still runs a tight ship, doesn't she?

CRAWFORD   I always knew I'd end up with a disciplinarian.

ALAN   The Tynes' own Third Reich. [*pauses*] Wouldn't you like that, Hen? You say "Jump," I say "How fuckin' high?"

CRAWFORD   Alright, brother. Take it down a notch.

ALAN   [*laughs*] I can't even take the trash out.

HEN   We should get to the table.

ALAN   Bullshit. It's only five.

[*Alan finishes the wine and pours himself another glass. Then, RISING, he drags himself over to the coffee table, picks up a knife, and begins to HACK AWAY AT A HUNK OF CHEESE.*]

CRAWFORD   [*quietly*] Give the poor bastard a chance, Alan.

ALAN   I missed having us together, Craw.

[*Crawford's expression is blank. He doesn't understand.*]

ALAN   It just wasn't the same over there without family.

[*CRACK. That sound again. Alan FLINCHES VIOLENTLY, this time with the knife in his hand. Crawford quickly grabs his arm.*]

CRAWFORD   It's the wind, Alan. Relax. [*pleading*] Please relax.

ALAN   [*angry*] That isn't the fucking wind. You wouldn't know. [*beat*] You weren't there. You were already home.

[*Alan DROPS THE KNIFE TO THE PLATE, where it CLATTERS. He swallows the rest of his wine with one long swig. Then, becoming aware of a song on the radio, he CROSSES unsteadily to it, and turns up the volume. The song "A HOLLY JOLLY CHRISTMAS" rings out.*]

ALAN   I remember this from last year. [*pauses*] You missed a hell of a Christmas party, Craw. All the boys said you woulda loved it.

CRAWFORD   [*quietly*] Don't do this.

ALAN   It was a Holly Jolly Christmas. Best time of the fucking year. All the guards getting drunk on Blackwater's dime. That night, we heard all kinds of things. But we didn't care. It was the holidays, man. We didn't even notice when they came in the door.

[*Suddenly, Hen bounds out of her seat and stares her husband down.*]

HEN   This is not the time. It's our family holiday. Listen to your brother.

ALAN   So what should we talk about, Hen?

HEN   [*quietly*] Nothing. [*beat*] Let's eat dinner.

ALAN   It's not time for dinner yet. Where's the whiskey, Leyenne?

LEYENNE   [*coldly*] I think Hen's right. We should eat. Not drink.

ALAN   [*fuming*] This is my house. Between these walls, I'm free to do what I want. I asked you where the whiskey is.

[*Leyenne hesitates, then pulls a bottle of whiskey from her bag. Alan snatches it from her aggressively and pours measures into four empty glasses. He drinks his, then passes the other glasses around. Hen rejects her glass.*]

HEN It's going to ruin dinner.

ALAN [*slurred*] Fuck dinner. Fuck this holiday. [*taking a swig*] All this goddamn commercialization. It's bullshit. . . . some corporate bigwig extorting us to buy a poor, overstuffed turkey pumped with additives for seventy percent profit margins. When we were boys, this holiday used to mean something.

HEN Don't ruin this, Alan. It's tradition.

ALAN [*contemptuous*] People like you are even worse, Hen. Buying into all this stupid shit. [*gestures to room*] All these fucking decorations. In Mogadishu, we didn't decorate anything. We sat around, and drank. And we thanked the Lord we were still alive. It meant twice as much as all this shit. Craw remembers.

LEYENNE [*coldly*] Hen spent a lot of time on decorating, Alan. So did Crawford. He did our whole house. It's tradition.

ALAN [*scoffs*] What a fucking surprise. Crawford doing your goddamn bidding. Haven't you gotten tired of playing with your puppet in twenty years, Leyenne?

HEN [*quietly*] Stop it. Stop it now. Put the whiskey down.

ALAN I'm fine.

HEN Fine? People who are fine don't ram into cars that cut them off. That kid's parents have a heartbeat monitor as a Christmas carol.

ALAN [*snarls*] Go ahead and use that language on the stand, sweetie. You won't have to watch me drink for a long stretch.

[*Hen is transformed. She is on her feet and furious, staring down her husband.*]

HEN You trapped yourself in this house! Don't you dare blame me.

CRAWFORD [*icily*] C'mon, no more of this.

HEN We don't need your sympathy, Crawford.

CRAWFORD [*angry*] This was never about sympathy. This was about celebration.

HEN [*laughs coldly*] Celebration? What exactly did we come here to celebrate? Is it that you made it out of that Somalian shithole before it did any permanent damage? Because not everyone was as goddamn lucky.

[*CRACK. THE SOUND AGAIN. A furious Alan leaps up, STRIDES to the door, and YANKS IT OPEN.*]

ALAN [*yelling out*] Come and get me, motherfuckers! I'm not guilty yet!

[*Alan BURSTS onto the PORCH. A FURIOUS BEEPING, like an alarm, rings out from his leg. Crawford CHASES HIM DOWN and GRABS HIM.*]

CRAWFORD [*pleading*] You have to stop this, Alan! We aren't in Mogadishu anymore! You need to learn to trust this world. . . .

ALAN Christmas was about you and me. [*verge of tears*] They tortured me in that goddamn desert, Crawford. You were supposed to protect me.

CRAWFORD We shouldn't have been there in the first place.

ALAN I needed the money.

CRAWFORD I thought I did too. But not as much as my wife needed me at home.

[*Alan sinks to the ground. Slowly, he pulls the leg of his pants up to reveal a HEAVY METAL BRACELET. This is what's BEEPING. Alan is on HOUSE ARREST. He massages his leg as the FAINT SOUNDS OF SIRENS can be heard.*]

ALAN This thing is so heavy. [*quietly*] It was terrible. Being in that cell, waiting for them to come back. [*beat*] But nothing was as bad as being alone.

[*A concerned Hen CROSSES TO THE DOORWAY.*]

CRAWFORD [*to Hen*] I got him, Hen. I got him this time.

[*Hen nods. Crawford WALKS OUT into the yard.*]

ALAN [*weakly*] Where are you going?

CRAWFORD You're already outside, Alan. [*beat*] Let's go build a goddamn snowman.

[*Alan slowly GETS TO HIS FEET and hobbles after his brother, who puts his arm around his shoulder and leads him on. As they DISAPPEAR INTO THE DARKNESS, the SOUND OF SIRENS becomes LOUDER.*]

FADE TO BLACK

END OF PLAY

Against the Clock

BY JACK LIVINGSTON

Copyright © by Jack Livingston. All rights reserved. Published with permission from the author. Inquiries concerning rights should be addressed to Jack Livingston at jackhlivingston@gmail.com.

Against the Clock

Presented October 3, 2014 | Swain Hall, Studio 6 Theatre, UNC Department of Communication | Directed by Carnessa Ottelin

CHARACTERS

Original cast members are in brackets.

CALVIN BOZEMAN 48, male. A former pro-football lineman with an imposing frame and voice [Michael Goolsby].

TEDY MCNEILL 46, male. A former pro-football defensive back, on the short side [Mark Jantzen].

TIME & SETTING

Present. Arlington, Virginia.

LIGHTS UP

On CALVIN BOZEMAN'S house. A display case with various football trophies is visible. Beside it hangs a framed Pro Bowl jersey. CALVIN sits in a chair, holding a hammer. He is wearing shorts and a worn T-shirt. At the foot of his chair is a drawer from a bedroom dresser. It's broken, with the wood on the sides chipped and ripped off. Next to Calvin is an open toolbox. He inspects the drawer before DRIVING A NAIL into the frame. TEDY MCNEILL ENTERS through the open front door. He is wearing a polo shirt and khakis. Calvin looks up from his project, is startled by Tedy's presence.

CALVIN [*spooked*] Oh. Tedy, you got me.

TEDY Sorry. The door was open. I didn't mean to scare you.

CALVIN [*regaining his composure, joking*] Hey, I didn't say, "You scared me." Pssh. You scaring me, string bean? I've dropped change that weighs more than you.

[*Calvin stands and lays the hammer on top of the wooden frame.*]

TEDY [*amused*] Why was the door open?

CALVIN I was just out, picking up groceries, running errands, you know. I probably just left it like that. How are you doing? It's great to see you.

TEDY I'm doing really well. It's great to see you too.

CALVIN [*beat*] So, what's the occasion?

TEDY I don't live far. Why not pop in?

CALVIN [*beat*] Well. Come on, make yourself comfortable.

[*Tedy takes a seat. Calvin picks up his hammer and returns to his work. The two are vis-à-vis. Calvin effortlessly sends ANOTHER NAIL INTO THE DRAWER with one quick motion.*]

CALVIN You know what I was just thinking abou. . . .

TEDY [*re: the drawer*] So, what's that? [*realizing he's cut him off*] Sorry. What were you saying?

CALVIN Nah, it's fine. I come into the bedroom one day, and this drawer looked like this. So, I decided I'd make a project out of it.

TEDY How did it happen?

CALVIN I guess the cleaning lady? I'm still confused how she'd even go about doing it. It's pretty beat up.

TEDY Jesus, man. You think it's her?

CALVIN I don't know who else it would be. She was doing me a favor, though. It was old, and when you'd try to open it, you would have to wiggle it out. Now, I can fix it and I have something to keep me busy, so. . . . a win-win.

TEDY Well, you should probably still ask her about it.

CALVIN [*offhandedly*] Yeah, sure.

[*Calvin inspects the drawer.*]

TEDY So, how close are you to being done?

[*Calvin views the piece.*]

CALVIN I guess I just need to reattach the runners.

[*Calvin turns the drawer over in his hands a few times.*]

TEDY I mean if it's old, you might want to get a professional to work on it. So it won't break. [*beat*] But whatever, it's great to see you in such good spirits.

CALVIN Yeah, I mean. . . .

[*Calvin stops hammering and gazes at Tedy.*]

CALVIN Wait, good spirits?

TEDY Nothing. Don't worry about it.

CALVIN No, good spirits. What do you mean?

TEDY It's. . . . last time we hung out, you kind of flew off the handle. It's really nothing. What were you going to say?

CALVIN Flew off the handle? When was that?

TEDY God, Calvin. It's nothing to get worked up over.

CALVIN [*playfully*] Nah. What was it? Was it about Millie?

TEDY No. Let's just forget I said. . . .

CALVIN Was it about the new coach? I told everyone he was garbage from day one. You go from Coach Cozza to this guy. Straight garbage.

TEDY Really, Cal, it's not a big deal. What were you going to say before I cut you off?

[*Calvin inspects the drawer again.*]

TEDY Calvin?

[*Calvin looks up.*]

CALVIN Wait, go back. What was the question?

TEDY What were you going to say to me before?

CALVIN When?

TEDY When I first got here.

CALVIN [*long beat*] I don't remember anymore. [*RISING*] I'm getting a beer. Want one?

TEDY I think I'm....

[*Calvin EXITS stage right. Tedy waits patiently. Calvin returns with two cans of soda. He hands one to Tedy, picks up his hammer, and sits back in his seat.*]

CALVIN This is all I had. I forgot I was running low on supplies.

TEDY You didn't pick any up when you were out earlier?

CALVIN We can run out and get some beer right now if you want.

[*Calvin takes a seat. Tedy puts his can by his feet.*]

TEDY No, it's fine. Any luck remembering what you were saying before? [*beat*] You said you were thinking about something. Was it about....?

[*Calvin flips the hammer, so that the bottom half is pointed at Tedy.*]

CALVIN I've got it! It was the 2003 Super Bowl.

[*Tedy's smile fades.*]

TEDY Oh. What about it?

CALVIN You know! Diego Mitjanis kept getting up in my face, trying to talk trash, and he was wearing a visor so you kept. . . . [*chuckling*] and you kept saying to him, "Roll your windows down. [*letting out a hearty laugh*] Roll your windows down. I can't hear you."

[*Calvin mimes manually rolling down a car window.*]

[*Tedy lets out a FORCED LAUGH.*]

TEDY Ha, right.

[*Calvin, still chuckling, begins to work on his drawer again, mapping where to place the trim. He places a nail on the trim and holds it in place.*]

CALVIN Two plays later you jump that screen, up from behind him and just suplex him backwards.

[*Calvin reels his hand back and brings it down hard on the nail. BOOM!*]

TEDY [*flat*] Yeah. I remember.

[*Tedy shifts uncomfortably in his seat. Calvin notices.*]

CALVIN What?

TEDY That was the only Super Bowl he was in. He barely played a set of downs.

CALVIN Yeah. You got him out of the game. You did what you were supposed to do. You set the tone.

TEDY All I'm saying is I wouldn't have hit someone that way if I knew it would do that to them.

CALVIN So, wait. If you could go back in time you would have kept their best player in the game? What if we lost?

TEDY Cal, I shouldn't have done that.

CALVIN [*incredulous*] What are you talking about? That's how you play the game.

[*Calvin points the hammer at Tedy.*]

CALVIN [*gruff*] You were the most vicious guy on that field....

TEDY Nothing's different. Relax, and don't point that at me.

CALVIN "Nothing's different"? You're soft.

TEDY I used to play with a chip on my shoulder. My whole life I was told that I was too small to play in the NFL. Back then I thought I had to prove them wrong, but it's not about toughness anymore.

CALVIN It's always been about toughness. How do you think I got here? I came from nothing. It was just me and my dad in the Virginia Beach projects. When I was twelve, this high school bully took my basketball at the park, and I came back crying. So my dad brings me back to the park, and we go over and the kid's playing with my ball. My dad tells me to get it....

TEDY Calvin....

[*Calvin's voice grows LOUDER.*]

CALVIN So I try to take the ball and run, but my dad won't let me. He pushes me back in. I'm fighting this kid six years older than me. I got trashed, but every time I tried to quit, my dad would be there pushing me back into the fight. How do you think I got this far? First-round pick, three-time All-Pro? You think that just happens?

TEDY Let's talk about this. Put the hammer down.

CALVIN [*belligerent*] You're not my therapist! Since that day nobody pushes me around. Why do you think CJ is playing at Tech this fall? He inherited his dad's tough genes. He was raised tough like his old man.

TEDY Well, maybe that's why he's afraid of you. CJ was at my camp. You know....

CALVIN Why are you here, Tedy?

TEDY I asked CJ about you. He's a good kid.

CALVIN Tell me why you're here.

TEDY I know you love him. I know you weren't always like this. You talk about being tough, but you would never hurt anyone when we played. I told him that.

CALVIN My son sent you?

TEDY No.

CALVIN Then why? You're here to tell me my son's afraid of me?

TEDY Cal. . . .

CALVIN I'll say it one more time. If you won't tell me why you came, then get out.

TEDY I can't do it when you're like this.

CALVIN [*trying to relax*] Tell me why you're here or leave.

TEDY Cal, Flip's dead. [*beat*] He couldn't create new memories, and he was just getting angry every day. I'd seen him a few days before. It was his head. He couldn't even find his way home.

CALVIN No, that's not true.

TEDY I wouldn't lie to you. Here. . . .

[*Tedy reaches into his front pants pocket and produces a slip of paper.*]

CALVIN Then how did he do it?

[*Tedy offers the slip of paper to Calvin.*]

TEDY That really doesn't matter. This has the info for where the service is. It's Friday. Take it.

[*Calvin takes the paper, puts it in his pocket.*]

CALVIN No, no. You're playing with my head. I want to know how he did it.

TEDY He shot himself in the chest. [*long beat*] He was hurting his family. He got kicked out of the house. You know how much he cared about them. He would just lose it. You know he wouldn't have done that. Cal, your family cares about you, too. [*beat*] I'm here because CJ's worried.

CALVIN Stop, that's not me. [*shaking his head*] Nah. Flip didn't do that. I mean, in the chest?

TEDY He did.

CALVIN Someone shot him, right? Made it look like a suicide. You shoot yourself in the head.

TEDY He wanted his brain to be used for research.

[*Calvin RISES with the hammer in his hand.*]

CALVIN [*bitterly*] No. Just no. Get out!

TEDY Calvin, put that down. I want you to come with me to see someone.

CALVIN I'm not seeing shit.

TEDY This is how we ended last week.

CALVIN [*beat*] You were here last week?

TEDY I've been here every week, Cal.

CALVIN [*defeated*] I said. . . . I said leave!

[*Calvin gestures to the door and looks away from Tedy. After a beat, Tedy RISES and CROSSES to the door. Stopping at the frame, he turns back.*]

TEDY I'm going to see you Friday at the service. A bunch of us are going to get you help.

CALVIN Well, then I'm not going.

[*Tedy pauses for a moment, then EXITS. Calvin sinks into his seat, despondent. He runs his hands through his hair. A beat later, he feels the paper in his pocket and takes it out. He reads it, inspects it curiously. He picks up the phone, dials a number using the paper as a consult, and puts the phone to his ear.*]

CALVIN Hello. . . . I have this paper. Is there a service at two on Friday? Who is that for? [*long beat as he listens*] Oh.

[*As Calvin attempts to piece together the information, the LIGHTS. . . .*]

FADE TO BLACK

END OF PLAY

Death and Dignity

BY SCHYLER HOPE MARTIN

Copyright © by Schyler Hope Martin. All rights reserved. Published with permission from the author. Inquiries concerning rights should be addressed to Schyler Hope Martin at schylermartin@gmail.com.

Death and Dignity

Presented October 23, 2015 | Kenan Theatre, UNC Department of Dramatic Art | Directed by Dana Coen

CHARACTERS
Original cast members are in brackets.

MICHAEL 62, male, pathologist. Husband to the late Catherine. Dedicated to his job, but far more dedicated to his wife [Michael Shannon].

CATHERINE 59, female, recently deceased. She's Michael's wife, sassy, fabulous, sharp, and intelligent [Jane Holding].

MILLIE [Voice] 30s, female, Michael's assistant [Mackenzie Kwok].

TIME & SETTING
Present. A small Southern town.

LIGHTS UP

On a medical examiner's room. The stage is stark and dimly lit. The space feels small, intimate. MICHAEL is alone and arranging surgical instruments on a table. He's wearing a white doctor's coat. A BODY, covered with a thin white sheet, lies on the examination table. A pair of female feet stick out from under the sheet. Michael glances nervously at the body, then sighs, peers under the sheet, and begins DICTATING into his smartphone.

MICHAEL The refrigerated body is that of a developed female, appearing the reported fifty-nine years of age. The body measures seventy inches and weighs one hundred sixty pounds. [*leaning in*]

The neck is symmetric and without masses. The chest is symmetric, and the breasts are free of palpable masses. [*lifting the lower corner of the sheet*] The genitalia are those of a normally developed adult woman.

[*CATHERINE APPEARS out of the shadows of the stage.*]

MICHAEL There is no evidence of injury. The vulva is. . . .

CATHERINE That's quite enough about my vulva, Michael. Thank you!

[*Catherine, a LIVING REPRESENTATION of the body on the table, is fully clothed. She wears a flattering dress. Her graying hair is perfectly styled. As Michael and Catherine converse, she speaks and moves naturally around him. MICHAEL ADDRESSES THE BODY ON THE TABLE as if he can't see Catherine's physical manifestation. He doesn't look shocked, but rather appears weary, resigned to this conversation.*]

MICHAEL It's my job, Catherine.

CATHERINE Surely we can skip the bit about [*a breathy whisper*] that.

[*A single tear forms in one of Michael's eyes as his emotions peek through.*]

CATHERINE Oh, don't look like that, Michael, dear. You knew this was coming.

MICHAEL It's. . . . it's nice to see you. Even like this. [*beat*] Did you call me "dear"?

CATHERINE I think I did. Maybe death has made me soft? [*beat*] You look like shit. I'm dead, and I still look better than you.

MICHAEL Fair enough.

CATHERINE How was my funeral? Did Eliza show up? Great heifer of a woman. If she did go, it was only because she was hoping to see Pastor Stu. As if he would ever give her the time of day. Doesn't she know he's already on his knees every evening? [*beat*] Not with prayer, of course. With Wallace, the organ player. A regular Romeo and Juliet, those two. . . . Romeo and Romeo? No matter.

MICHAEL   Jesus, Catherine. Death hasn't made you soft.

CATHERINE   It's just death. It's not an emotional awakening.

MICHAEL   Let me get on with this. Don't want them thinking I can't handle it.

CATHERINE   Cutting open your dead wife? It does seem unprofessional.

MICHAEL   It's a small town. Who else was going to do it?

[*Michael picks up a SCALPEL from the table beside him and moves his hands under the sheet as if he were CUTTING into the body. Catherine watches him closely.*]

MICHAEL   I miss you.

CATHERINE   I wasn't much fun in the end. All work, really. I was dependent on everyone. . . . on you. You couldn't have enjoyed that.

MICHAEL   No, but it was better than not having you at all.

CATHERINE   Was it?

MICHAEL   [*adamant*] Yes. It was. [*beat*] It's your presence, I think. The house is so quiet now.

CATHERINE   You used to complain about how loud I was.

MICHAEL   I do stand by that. [*peering under the sheet, DICTATING*] The strap muscles, larynx, cartilages, and cervical vertebral column are unremarkable.

CATHERINE   Are you watering the petunias?

MICHAEL   That's what you're worried about?

CATHERINE   I worked hard to get those petunias growing the way they do.

MICHAEL I'm watering them.

CATHERINE Good. Very good.

MICHAEL [*DICTATING*] The stomach is of usual size. [*long beat*] The mucosa displays unusual patterns. Your stomach lining is mottled. Unnaturally so. This doesn't seem to have come from the cancer.

CATHERINE A side effect of the treatment, perhaps?

MICHAEL No, this is something different. It looks almost like. . . .

CATHERINE How many people cried at the funeral? How many people *pretended* to cry? That's a very important thing to distinguish. I can hold a grudge, even in the afterlife.

[*Michael isn't paying attention to her.*]

MICHAEL Doesn't make any sense.

CATHERINE [*rattling on*] The treatment was harsh, would've mottled anyone's stomach! [*an afterthought*] Maybe not Eliza's, that moose of a woman. She's impenetrable. The devil himself wouldn't touch her with a ten-foot pole. Did you know that she once. . . .

MICHAEL [*strongly*] CATHERINE, PLEASE! [*beat*] I need to focus!

[*Catherine falls silent. A soft KNOCK on the door.*]

MILLIE [*offstage*] Everything all right in there?

MICHAEL [*with forced composure*] Just fine, Millie.

MILLIE [*offstage*] I thought I heard you saying something.

MICHAEL Dictating the autopsy. Thank you, Mills.

[*Catherine's eyes widen. She mouths "Mills??" and makes a dramatic gagging motion.*]

MILLIE [*offstage*] Of course. Anything you need, Michael. You let me know.

CATHERINE [*beat*] Well! I've certainly never felt more like a third wheel in my life.

MICHAEL You're dead. You're not allowed to be jealous.

CATHERINE Did you seriously call her "Mills"? That's cringe-worthy. I tried to get you to call me Cathy for years, but nooo. I always looked like more of a "classic Catherine." At best I'd get Cath. And that's when you were feeling lazy.

MICHAEL You are more of a classic Catherine. [*wincing a bit*] Were.

CATHERINE She sounds cute though. I'll give you that. And young.

MICHAEL She's a coworker.

CATHERINE Not a friend? [*beat*] She could be a friend. You need friends in a dark time like this.

MICHAEL You're patronizing me.

CATHERINE Not at all. You have to move forward eventually.

MICHAEL Your body's still warm.

CATHERINE Impossible. It's been days since I died.

MICHAEL It's an expression.

CATHERINE [*continuing on*] Michael and Millie. . . . has a nice ring to it.

MICHAEL Stop, Catherine. Please. Let me get back to my job. [*leaning back in*] These injuries are not consistent with a death from cancer.

CATHERINE It was stage four. There is no stage five, you know.

MICHAEL This kind of inflammation wouldn't come from cancer at any stage.

CATHERINE Perhaps it could come from. . . .

MICHAEL [*YELLING as he interrupts*] NO! No, Catherine! This is NOT the goddamn cancer!

[*Michael's face is red. He's breathing heavily.*]

CATHERINE [*long beat, then quietly*] Yes, I know. Of course I know.

MICHAEL But *I* didn't.

[*Michael puts down his instruments and takes a step away from her body. He collects himself before speaking again.*]

MICHAEL You killed yourself, took a handful of pills, didn't you? [*wearily*] And don't try to distract me anymore. We've arrived at the truth, and I think we ought to stay here.

CATHERINE [*heavy beat of silence*] I was dying either way.

MICHAEL Maybe you weren't.

CATHERINE Of course I was. [*beat*] I opted for. . . . What is it they're calling it. . . . death with dignity?

MICHAEL Dignity's got nothing to do with it. You took the easy way out. Did you even think about what this would do to me?

CATHERINE It wasn't about you!

MICHAEL No! It wasn't! But you know what? [*beat*] Maybe it should have been.

CATHERINE [*coldly*] I'm terribly sorry for the inconvenience my death has caused you.

MICHAEL You could have told me, Cath. I would have been with you, beside you at the end. You didn't have to be alone. I. . . . I wouldn't have been angry.

[*Now it's Catherine who looks sad.*]

MICHAEL I would have held your hand. If you'd told me.

CATHERINE [*contrite*] I'm sorry I didn't tell you, Michael. [*long beat*] You take your time joining me, all right? I don't mind the wait.

MICHAEL [*fighting his emotions*] Careful, Cath. You're almost being sweet.

[*Catherine smiles and wrinkles her nose.*]

CATHERINE Don't embarrass me during my own autopsy. [*beat*] And don't you forget to water those petunias.

MICHAEL Still worried about the damn petunias.

CATHERINE I care a lot about my petunias. I want them taken care of.

[*Michael nods. This isn't really about flowers. He reflects on her statement for a moment.*]

MICHAEL I'll take care of them. [*beat, then DICTATING*] Cause of death.... Intentional overdose.... Suicide.

[*Catherine falls silent. MICHAEL REACHES FOR THE BODY'S HAND from beneath the sheet. SIMULTANEOUSLY, CATHERINE REACHES OUT FOR HIM as if it were her hand he's holding. After a satisfied moment, she turns and DISAPPEARS BACK INTO THE SHADOWS. Michael holds the body's hand gently, as if it means the whole world to him. He then stares straight out into the audience.... and his future.*]

FADE TO BLACK

END OF PLAY

Shot through the Heart

BY JENNIFER MORGAN

Copyright © by Jennifer Morgan. All rights reserved. Published with permission from the author. Inquiries concerning rights should be addressed to Jennifer Morgan at jaykmo@gmail.com.

Shot through the Heart

Premiered October 6, 2011 | Swain Hall, Studio 6 Theatre, UNC Department of Communication | Directed by Joseph Megel

CHARACTERS

Original cast members are in brackets.

A.D. 30s, the assistant director [Marietta Braye].

CAMERON 30s, female. A veteran actress, plays MAGGIE on the series [Celina Chapman].

HANNAH 20s, female. She's just getting her start as an actress on a television series, plays JO, a Brooklyn cop [Haley Scruggs].

JEREMY 50s, male. A veteran actor, plays the CHIEF, Jo's father [Estes Tarver].

TIME & SETTING

Present. The sets and dressing room of a television series.

SCENE ONE

LIGHTS UP

On an exterior street set. HANNAH [as JO] and CAMERON [as MAGGIE] face each other at center stage. Cameron has her arms crossed and is looking intently at Hannah, who is confused and hurt. The A.D. STEPS IN with a slate. The show's THEME SONG IS HEARD. This differentiates the show from the "real world."

A.D. *Shot through the Heart,* season one, episode three: "Partners." Action!

[*The A.D. EXITS.*]

MAGGIE The hell were you thinking, rookie?

JO You would've died!

MAGGIE So you'd rather throw away your life instead?

JO I was wearing Kevlar.

MAGGIE Right. And I was out there in bubble wrap.

JO Look, I wasn't thinking, all right? It seemed like the right thing to do.

MAGGIE No, the right thing to do would be to watch out for your own ass and let me do the same. You take enough bullets in this job without taking them for everybody else, too.

JO Lesson learned. Next time a shooter has you in his sights, I'll let him put a slug in you.

[*Jo turns to leave, but Maggie grabs her arm and forces Jo to face her. She does not let go for the rest of their conversation.*]

MAGGIE You'd better.

JO Let go of me.

MAGGIE I know a bleeding heart when I see one. You didn't take that bullet for me. You took it so you wouldn't have to shoot.

JO [*looking down*] That's not. . . .

MAGGIE Look at me!

[*Jo does.*]

MAGGIE If you had time to jump in front of me, you had time to drop him. Instead, you let him get a shot off. You got lucky this time, but what happens when you're on patrol with no vest? Or if the next guy is smart enough to aim for your head, huh? If you see a perp pull a gun, don't even think about me. Shoot. Otherwise, I'll find a partner who will.

JO [*under her breath*] If you can.

MAGGIE What was that?

JO I've heard all about your track record with partners. We both know I'm your last chance.

MAGGIE Big words from the little girl who's only on the force because her daddy's the chief.

JO [*momentarily stunned into silence*] Why do you hate me so much?

[*For a moment, they just stare at each other. Then, suddenly, Maggie KISSES Jo. After some hesitation, Jo returns the kiss, but it's forced.*]

A.D. [*offstage*] Cut! Take five, everyone!

END OF SCENE

SCENE TWO

[*Hannah and Cameron ENTER the dressing room to get ready for the next shot. Cameron looks at Hannah like she wants to say something, but Hannah is facing the opposite direction. After deliberating, Cameron speaks.*]

CAMERON [*smiling*] First time?

HANNAH [*startled*] Huh?

CAMERON First on-screen kiss, I mean.

HANNAH Was it that obvious?

CAMERON Let me put it this way. . . . you reminded me of myself. The first time I did a make-out scene, it was, and I quote, "like kissing a goat."

HANNAH What does that even mean?

CAMERON I didn't get it at first, but trust me, you'll know right away if it happens to you.

HANNAH Sorry, it's just....

CAMERON Hey, no need to apologize. Believe me, I understand. Just do better next time.

HANNAH I'll try.

CAMERON Not good enough. [*checking her watch*] Yeah, we've got time.

HANNAH For what?

[*Cameron steps up to Hannah, so close that their noses are almost touching.*]

CAMERON Kiss me.

HANNAH [*backing away*] I don't....

[*Cameron follows, putting her hands firmly on Hannah's shoulders.*]

CAMERON No buts. Shut up and kiss me.

HANNAH Cameron....

CAMERON Hannah. If you can't even kiss me here, alone, how are you going to do it in front of America? You've got to get inside your character's head. Jo took a bullet for Maggie. When you kiss me, I have to know that you'd die for me.... If you can do that, everything else will fall into place.

[*Hannah takes a deep, shaky breath, then PRESSES HER LIPS to Cameron's. The kiss starts off soft, but quickly becomes passionate. Their costar JEREMY ENTERS and spots them. He takes a moment to enjoy the show.*]

JEREMY [*grinning*] I think your threesome is missing something.

[*The women break apart, startled. Cameron recovers first, while Hannah looks mortified.*]

CAMERON The goat left early.

[*Hannah giggles nervously at the joke; Jeremy doesn't get it, but he's willing to play along.*]

JEREMY His loss. Can I be of assistance?

CAMERON Not today. [*putting her arm around Hannah's shoulder and speaking like her gruffer character, Maggie*] I think my partner and I have it covered, Chief.

JEREMY Alright, I get it. Just wanted to let you know they're ready to go again. [*winking*] Don't have too much fun without me.

[*He EXITS. Cameron breaks away from Hannah, but Hannah, having been affected by this moment, doesn't move.*]

CAMERON [*looking back at Hannah as she begins to exit*] You ready to do this?

HANNAH [*snapping out of it, nodding*] Yeah. Of course.

[*They EXIT together.*]

END OF SCENE

SCENE THREE

[*Hannah ENTERS and crosses to center stage. The A.D. STEPS IN with a slate. The THEME SONG plays.*]

A.D. *Shot through the Heart*, season one, episode fourteen: "Lovers." Action!

[*The A.D. EXITS. Hannah, as JO, crosses the stage to the CHIEF'S office. We hear the faint sound of MOANING, clothes rustling, etc. She knocks on the door; no answer.*]

JO [*as she opens the door*] Dad, we need to....

[*We hear the sound of CONFUSED/SURPRISED VOICES, one male and the other female, FROM OFFSTAGE. Jo's eyes widen. Stunned, she turns away and CROSSES AWAY, her hand over her mouth. Cameron, as MAGGIE, exits the office, adjusting her disheveled clothing, followed closely by Jeremy, as the CHIEF. Jo does not turn to face them.*]

MAGGIE Oh my God! Jo....

CHIEF Jo....

JO [*disgusted*] How could you?

CHIEF Now, listen....

JO [*turning quickly to face him*] Chief, *Sir*, I think it would be best if we didn't discuss this here.

CHIEF Discuss this? I'm your father and your superior. We don't discuss my personal life at all.

JO We do when you're sexually harassing my partner.

CHIEF I'm only going to say this once; drop it.

JO And if I don't?

MAGGIE [*cutting in*] Chief! Let me talk to her. I'll get this sorted out.

[*A beat as the CHIEF glances between the two women. Then, without a word, he EXITS.*]

JO This is why you've been coming in early?

MAGGIE Jo....

JO I mean, I knew you didn't want anyone to see us coming in together, but this.... [*beat*] Do you love him?

MAGGIE [*looking away*] No.

JO Then how could you do this to me?

MAGGIE He's been coming on to me since I started here. I finally just....

[*She shrugs halfheartedly.*]

JO What is he to you? Are you screwing your way to the top?

MAGGIE Don't you dare!

JO Wait, I have a better question. What am I to you?

MAGGIE Oh, not this again.

JO I'm serious. It's been three months, and I've never even been to your apartment. I haven't met any of your friends. I haven't met your mom or.... [*realizing*] No telling the parents, huh?

MAGGIE You're not exactly the kind of person you bring home to meet the folks. Not *my* folks, anyway.

JO And what's wrong with me?

MAGGIE Oh, I have a whole list, but "not a man" is definitely in the top three.

JO Well, my dad certainly doesn't have that problem. Will he be coming around for Christmas dinner?

MAGGIE Don't.

JO Just tell me. Am I your girlfriend? Your lover? What?

MAGGIE Whatever this is, it's good. Don't screw it up by trying to make it into something it's not.

JO Maggie....

MAGGIE I'll see you on patrol.

A.D. [*offstage*] Cut! Great work, everyone!

[*Hannah and Cameron EXIT.*]

END OF SCENE

SCENE FOUR

[*Cameron and Hannah ENTER the dressing room together.*]

HANNAH They're really writing him off?

CAMERON Jeremy's got a new pilot.

HANNAH Something about the devil, right? Talk about typecasting.

CAMERON Ouch! I don't think he's that bad.

HANNAH Last week, he called me by name for the first time. The name he used was Sally.

CAMERON Okay, he might be that bad.

HANNAH I'm glad he's leaving. We won't miss him.

CAMERON [*laughing*] Tell me how you really feel.

[*After a reflective beat, Hannah chooses to do just that.*]

HANNAH [*mustering*] Okay, I. . . .

A.D. [*peeking her head in the door*] Let's get back to it, everyone!

CAMERON [*to the A.D.*] Thank you.

[*Cameron EXITS. After a disappointed moment, Hannah follows.*]

END OF SCENE

SCENE FIVE

[*The A.D. STEPS IN with a slate. Jeremy (as the CHIEF), Cameron (as MAGGIE), and Hannah (as JO) ENTER.*]

A.D. *Shot through the Heart,* season one, episode fifteen: "Christmas Dinner."

[*Maggie, Jo, and the chief sit uncomfortably opposite one another at a dinner table.*]

A.D. *Shot through the Heart,* season one, episode nineteen: "The New Chief."

[*THE THREE CHANGE POSES. The CHIEF now LIES DEAD on the ground. Hannah and Cameron look on, horrified.*]

A.D. *Shot through the Heart,* season one, episode twenty-three: "Officer Down, Part One."

[*Jeremy EXITS, while Cameron and Hannah CHANGE POSES. They stand center stage, guns drawn, staring intently offscreen. Cameron is behind Hannah and well outside of her line of sight.*]

A.D. *Shot through the Heart,* season one, episode twenty-four, season finale: "Officer Down, Part Two." Action!

[*The A.D. EXITS. Sound of SIRENS, GUNSHOTS, INDISTINCT SHOUTING, and the SHOW'S THEME, all overlapping chaotically; then, silence. Cameron, as MAGGIE, hits the ground, hard. Hannah, as JO, FIRES THREE TIMES in rapid succession. After a pause, she visibly relaxes.*]

JO [*turning to Maggie*] I got him.... [*seeing her*] Oh my God!

[*Jo drops to her knees and immediately tends to a bloody gunshot wound in Maggie's chest.*]

JO [*frantic whisper*] Damn it!

[*She applies pressure to the wound, but Maggie's fading.*]

JO [*SCREAMING offstage*] OFFICER DOWN! I need an ambulance here!

[*Jo and Maggie FREEZE. The MUSIC CUTS OFF. They RISE and EXIT.*]

END OF SCENE

SCENE SIX

[*Hannah ENTERS the dressing room. Her eyes are red and puffy. She's been crying. She looks at her hands and wipes what's on them off on her uniform. Cameron and Jeremy ENTER. Cameron APPROACHES. Jeremy hangs back.*]

CAMERON I can't believe you've been holding out on me like this! Seriously, where did that even come from? Hannah, that performance screamed "Emmy."

HANNAH Great.

CAMERON You okay?

HANNAH I'm fine.

[*She waits for a response, but a worried Cameron can only stare back.*]

HANNAH I guess I'm still a little shaken up.... [*beat*] I really got into Jo's head that time.

CAMERON Oh, trust me, we could all tell. I knew you had it in you.

HANNAH Are we doing another take?

CAMERON No, my friend, we are done! [*beat*] Well, *I'm* done. You've got at least another year of this left. I can't believe *Shot through the Heart* got renewed for a second season. [*realizing how tactless that sounds*] But, man, am I glad, for your sake, it did.

HANNAH Thanks. And congratulations on *Raising Hell*.

CAMERON Fingers crossed. Fox loves our chemistry, and the writing is fantastic. Plus, it's a sitcom about the Antichrist's stepmom; what's not to love? Really though, I'm just happy to be playing a straight character again. Between *Shot through the Heart* and the last series I did, I've been a lesbian for the last five years.

[*Jeremy slides his arms about Cameron's waist.*]

JEREMY Oh, yeah, acting like you're in love with me must be a huge challenge for you. The real question is, with a face like this, who'll believe me as Satan?

CAMERON I'm sure you'll manage.

JEREMY Only because you bring out the devil in me.

HANNAH Well, I'm really happy for you. For both of you.

JEREMY We're happy for us, too.

CAMERON Oh, stop it!

HANNAH So, are you off to celebrate?

CAMERON Do you really have to ask? What about you?

HANNAH I don't have anything planned.

CAMERON You can't fool me. I bet you have an adventure of your own cooked up. You're going to go crazy, aren't you? [*beat*] Seriously, though, go out and have fun tonight, okay? And take care of yourself. I'll worry when I'm not here to keep an eye on you.

[*Cameron hugs Hannah. Hannah hangs on a bit too long.*]

HANNAH I'm going to miss you.

CAMERON [*pulling away*] Don't worry, we'll keep in touch. I'll call you sometime, okay?

HANNAH Sure. Anytime.

JEREMY Take care of yourself, kid.

[*Waving, Cameron and Jeremy EXIT. Hannah's eyes remain trained on the closed door. After a long moment, she EXITS.*]

END OF SCENE

SCENE SEVEN

[*Hannah, as JO, and Cameron, as MAGGIE, ENTER and RESUME THEIR POSITIONS AT THE END OF SCENE FIVE.*]

JO [*SCREAMING offstage*] OFFICER DOWN! I need an ambulance here! [*to Maggie*] Don't do this to me!

[*She checks Maggie's pulse. When she feels nothing, she takes her hand off Maggie's chest and sits quietly for a beat.*]

JO No Kevlar, huh? Was it just today? You know better than to. . . .

[*She trails off, looking down at her hands. They have Maggie's blood on them.*]

JO I got him, though. The shooter. I put a bullet right between his eyes. I wasn't thinking about anything else, I was totally focused on him and the gun. I did exactly what I was supposed to do.

[*Jo STARTS TO CRY. The SOUND OF AN AMBULANCE can be heard offstage.*]

A.D. [*offstage*] Cut! That's a wrap!

[*Cameron BREAKS CHARACTER, STANDS, and looks back at Hannah with surprise to see that she's NOT DONE CRYING. After a concerned beat, Cameron decides to leave her be and EXITS.*]

[*The A.D. ENTERS and begins striking the scenery.*]

[*Hannah continues to stare at the spot where Cameron lay. Gazing at the blood on her hand, she continues to SOB.*]

FADE TO BLACK

END OF PLAY

The Rabbit

BY BROOKE ODOM

Copyright © by Brooke Odom. All rights reserved. Published with permission from the author. Inquiries concerning rights should be addressed to Brooke Odom at brookeodom1@gmail.com.

The Rabbit

The Rabbit was chosen for the 2011 inaugural season of Long Story Shorts, but remained unproduced because of resource issues. I wanted to honor its value, however, by including it in this collection. —Dana Coen

CHARACTERS

EVELYN 38, female.

GEORGE 28, male. Evelyn's husband.

JUSTINE 20, female. Maid.

TOMMY 68, male. Groundskeeper.

TIME & SETTING

June 26, 1937. A manor in Warwick, England.

SCENE ONE

LIGHTS UP

On EVELYN, standing in the center of an EMPTY STAGE. She is onstage the entire performance.

EVELYN [*to the audience*] "The greatest mysteries have death in them, but death itself has little mystery." I wrote that. As the best-known mystery writer in England, I thought it to be true.

[*GEORGE ENTERS with a Victorian chair. He sits, begins to smoke a pipe.*]

EVELYN As someone who is no longer living, I can now promise you that it is.

[*JUSTINE ENTERS with an antique desk. From the drawers she removes a duster and a newspaper, which she hands to George. She begins to clean the desk.*]

EVELYN In my books, the characters that die always misread the signs and warnings around them. While they are ultimately expendable, they are still fascinating. For who is warned of death and chooses to believe it a lie? And in death, what truth remains?

[*TOMMY ENTERS with a low parlor table, set across from the chair. He EXITS.*]

EVELYN I will show you my last day alive, and you will understand; death is not mysterious. But what blinds us to it. . . . there lies the mystery.

GEORGE Justine, is there any tea? I'm parched.

JUSTINE Yes, Sir. Right away.

EVELYN They were having an affair.

[*Justine EXITS. Evelyn turns from the audience and WALKS INTO THE SCENE.*]

GEORGE Morning, dear.

EVELYN Did you sleep well? I didn't feel you come to bed until after midnight.

GEORGE You know me, always up reading the trades. You're rested?

EVELYN Yes, thank you.

[*A kiss. Justine ENTERS with a tea tray, which she sets on the table. She begins to make tea.*]

EVELYN The papers will arrive today.

GEORGE   Good. I'll finally start to feel like your husband. [*to Justine*] Where is the cream?

JUSTINE   Oh, I must have left it in the kitchen. One moment, Sir.

[*Justine EXITS.*]

EVELYN   [*to the audience*] They were discreet. But his eyes.... [*to George*] I love you.

GEORGE   I love you too, darling.

[*A SCREAM offstage. Justine ENTERS IN A RUSH, panicked.*]

JUSTINE   Oh, that awful man. He's killed a.... there's blood all over the kitchen.

[*Tommy ENTERS. He carries a dead rabbit.*]

TOMMY   Mistress Evelyn, these animals still be getting in my vegetables day in and out. Chewed right through the wire and the fencing, like I told you they would. And now half my planting's gone to waste.

EVELYN   [*to the audience*] Tommy had worked this land for my father for twenty years, and then my first husband for ten more. He and the estate were inseparable.

GEORGE   So the animal.... You....

TOMMY   [*withdraws a handgun from his pocket*] Shot it.

[*Justine SCREAMS again and swoons into the chair. George fans her with his newspaper.*]

EVELYN   Tommy, for the last time, you cannot kill defenseless creatures on my property. Now put down that infernal weapon and get back to work.

[*Tommy TOSSES THE GUN onto the desk and STORMS off. Evelyn takes a breath and turns to George, who looks from the tea tray to Justine.*]

GEORGE Dammit, she forgot the cream.

END OF SCENE

SCENE TWO

[*Evelyn stands off, watching. The tea tray is gone. George stands alone and admires the gun. He shoves it quickly into a drawer as Justine enters.*]

JUSTINE I have a parcel. . . .

[*George eagerly grabs it from her hands and rips it open. He withdraws a thick sheaf of paper.*]

EVELYN [*to the audience*] The papers solidified his new earnings as my husband.

GEORGE Sixty millions pounds. . . .

JUSTINE Well, 30 million after the divorce.

GEORGE [*relishing*] Sixty million pounds. . . .

JUSTINE Now we can leave this horrid estate and that old woman.

GEORGE [*suddenly alert*] Justine. . . .

JUSTINE Yes, George?

GEORGE Did you hear the back door close?

[*Evelyn ENTERS THE SCENE as they spring apart.*]

EVELYN George, here you are. Justine, would you wipe down the desk, please? And then go out to the garden and pick some flowers for the room?

JUSTINE Yes, Madam.

[*Justine begins to clean the desk.*]

GEORGE Feeling better?

EVELYN   Yes, I am. I feel wonderful, actually.

GEORGE   I'll tell the cook no more porridge for breakfast.

[*Justine opens the drawer and removes the gun. She polishes it slowly, then puts it back.*]

EVELYN   And, it seems now I'll be getting ill quite often in the mornings. . . .

[*George looks at her expectantly.*]

EVELYN   George, I'm pregnant. We're going to have a child!

GEORGE   You're. . . .

EVELYN   You know how long I've wanted children. Isn't this wonderful?

GEORGE   [*a paralyzed beat*] I'll go put champagne in the icebox. After dinner we'll celebrate.

[*George CROSSES to Evelyn. He places a hand on her stomach and smiles. She glows.*]

GEORGE   To the future.

EVELYN   To the future.

[*They kiss and George EXITS. Justine is frozen.*]

EVELYN   Justine?

JUSTINE   Yes? Oh, I'm sorry.

EVELYN   The flowers. . . .

JUSTINE   Yes, I'll get those for you. Right away.

EVELYN   Is there anything else?

[*Justine stops.*]

JUSTINE   Congratulations, Madam.

EVELYN Thank you.

[*Justine EXITS with a curtsey.*]

END OF SCENE

SCENE THREE

[*Evelyn watches from off. A bouquet of flowers is on the table. George sits, smokes a pipe. Tommy ENTERS.*]

GEORGE I checked with the physician. He confirmed it.

TOMMY Inconvenient.

GEORGE You're sure she'll lose it?

TOMMY Aye. With the late Sir Havers, every time.

EVELYN [*to the audience*] If there was a child, he or she alone would inherit George's share of our money. George would receive nothing if we were to divorce.

TOMMY I'll still be getting my twenty percent.

GEORGE We decided fifteen.

TOMMY [*beat*] Georgie-boy, I don't recall you having the stomach to see this agreement all the way through, should it come to it. One way or another, I'm getting what's mine.

[*George decides not to push it.*]

TOMMY [*satisfied*] Now that's settled, I'd best be back to the garden. Where's my gun?

[*Tommy CROSSES to the desk.*]

GEORGE How should I know?

[*Tommy finds the gun in the drawer. Evelyn ENTERS THE SCENE.*]

EVELYN Dear, it's time for dinner.

[*Tommy SHOVES THE GUN back into the drawer.*]

EVELYN Oh, Tommy, your plate is in the kitchen. [*beat*] We're having rabbit.

[*She smiles.*]

END OF SCENE

SCENE FOUR

[*George sits in the chair with a large stain on his shirt. Evelyn wipes it with a soaked cloth.*]

GEORGE Bloody soup.

EVELYN The girl *is* rather clumsy. [*calls offstage*] Justine?

[*Justine ENTERS.*]

JUSTINE Here, Madam. [*to George*] I apologize again, Sir.

EVELYN The seltzer?

JUSTINE Are you sure it's in the pantry? I looked on the first shelf, and the second, and the third, and behind the door, and. . . .

EVELYN For heaven's sake, I'll get it. [*to the audience*] She'd begun to panic.

[*Evelyn CROSSES OUT OF THE SCENE.*]

JUSTINE [*upset*] A baby?!

GEORGE [*avoiding*] I'm going to change my shirt.

[*George EXITS. Tommy ENTERS. He retrieves the gun from the desk.*]

JUSTINE Again?

TOMMY Those damn creatures are going to be shown just whose land they're on.

[*Evelyn RE-ENTERS.*]

EVELYN Tommy, put it down.

TOMMY You'd sacrifice all my work for an animal you don't even know.

EVELYN That's enough.

[*George ENTERS.*]

GEORGE Tommy, what are you doing?

EVELYN He was just going to pack his things. He's released.

GEORGE [*beat*] Evelyn, I don't think....

EVELYN Someone else can manage the land. I appreciate what you've done for us, Tommy, but if you can't respect me I'm afraid our partnership must end.

TOMMY See, that's your mistake, Mistress.

GEORGE Tommy....

TOMMY I've worked this land over half my life. I'll never be moved off this property.

EVELYN Well, neither will I.

[*George CROSSES to stand in front of Evelyn.*]

GEORGE My dear, maybe you're just not thinking straight with the baby....

EVELYN George. I am perfectly reasonable.

TOMMY I will have what is rightfully mine.

[*Tommy advances, George holds up a hand.*]

GEORGE Give me the gun.

[*A beat. Tommy gives the gun to George. Evelyn hides her relief.*]

GEORGE Leave. Go pack up your shovels and tools.

[*Tommy pauses, then EXITS.*]

GEORGE Justine, go to the gate and tell John that Tommy will be leaving shortly. We'll call the police.

JUSTINE But. . . .

GEORGE Go.

[*Justine EXITS. George holds Evelyn.*]

EVELYN I thought. . . . for a moment I thought he really might try to. . . .

GEORGE But he didn't. Are you all right? The baby?

EVELYN Yes. . . . Thank you.

[*He brushes the hair back from her face.*]

GEORGE Evelyn, what if something were to happen. . . . to the child? If you couldn't. . . .

EVELYN No, this time. . . . it will live. I can feel it. I've even mailed a notice to my publisher. No more writing for now. Just us.

GEORGE You love me?

EVELYN More than anything.

GEORGE You'll never leave me?

EVELYN George. We'll always be together.

GEORGE Yes, I'll always have you with me. I love you.

[*Evelyn sees the flowers.*]

EVELYN Those need a vase. You'll ring the police?

[*George nods.*]

GEORGE Darling, do you want the gun?

EVELYN I can't bear to hold it. I keep thinking of what it's killed.

[*George nods in sympathy. As Evelyn turns to exit, HE RAISES IT AND POINTS IT AT HER.*]

END OF SCENE

SCENE FIVE

[*Evelyn stands on an empty stage. THE SOUNDS OF SHOVELING are heard.*]

EVELYN [*to the audience*] They're burying me in the garden.

[*The SHOVELING grows LOUDER.*]

EVELYN Never to be found, I'm sure. Tommy will have his land, George will have his money, and Justine will have George. It is always the characters. . . . the characters that are ultimately responsible for their fates. "Who killed me?" the dead want to ask. I would write the man holding the gun is responsible. But I gave it to him. He was never mine, just as this estate was never Tommy's and my child will never live. In the end, as every good character knows, there is only one person responsible for their death. And now I know it, too. [*barely audible*] It was me.

FADE TO BLACK

END OF PLAY

Amendment

BY RYAN PASSER

Copyright © by Ryan Passer. All rights reserved. Published with permission from the author. Inquiries concerning rights should be addressed to Ryan Passer at rpasser93@gmail.com.

Amendment

Presented October 3, 2014 | Swain Hall, Studio 6 Theatre, UNC Department of Communication | Directed by Dana Coen

CHARACTERS

Original cast members are in brackets.

JACK MORGAN Late 40s, male. Father of an incarcerated teenager [Michael Shannon].

REP. KENNETH RIVERS Mid-50s, male. Congressman and gun-rights supporter [Bill Garrity].

ARTHUR GILLIGAN Early 50s, male. Father of a comatose patient [Mark Jantzen].

TIME & SETTING

Present. A secluded room at a country club restaurant in the South.

LIGHTS UP

On the intimate back room of a country club restaurant. In the center of the stage rests a wooden table draped in fancy white tablecloth. On it sit glasses, napkins, and silverware. A few feet behind the table is a large window. Sitting at the left edge of the table is ARTHUR GILLIGAN. He STARES down at his glass with a distant gaze. At the right sits JACK MORGAN, who unconsciously TAPS the side of his plate with a spoon. Sitting in between the two at the back of the table is REPRESENTATIVE KENNETH RIVERS.

JACK It just felt. . . . wrong. I don't know how else to describe it. I had this giant knot in my stomach the whole time.

RIVERS Don't you enjoy visiting him?

JACK Of course I do. But I just. . . . God, I can't see him like that. So broken. He can't function in there.

RIVERS I know it's got to be rough for the boy. But believe me, I'm sure he appreciates seeing his dad.

JACK Maybe. It's just every time I think back to that look on his face in the courtroom, I just. . . .

[*As he trails off, Arthur glances up from the table.*]

ARTHUR What . . . ?

RIVERS [*pointing to Jack's spoon*] Mr. Gilligan. The spoon.

[*Jack HANDS the spoon to Arthur, who holds it with disinterest.*]

ARTHUR Listen, Mr. . . . . err, Representative. I don't know what you're supposed to call someone in the House.

RIVERS Mr. Rivers is perfectly acceptable.

ARTHUR Mr. Rivers, why are we doing this? If you wanted us to "discuss things" so much, wouldn't it be easier if we didn't have to pass around silverware?

RIVERS Conversation can be beneficial, Mr. Gilligan, but only when it's productive, when no one's getting attacked. The "speaking spoon" ensures that. Keeping things civilized is. . . .

[*As a skeptical Arthur waits for him to finish, Representative Rivers suddenly stops and inhales several times through his nose.*]

RIVERS Is it just me, or does it seem a little stuffy in here?

JACK If there's any ventilation, I'm not feeling it. Doesn't help that it's so damn cramped, either.

RIVERS Well, they did say it was the "coziest room in the restaurant." At least we've got plenty of privacy. When the waitress comes back, I'll ask her to turn on the air.

ARTHUR It took her fifteen minutes just to get our drink order.

RIVERS Well, here.... Why don't we just open up the window a bit?

[*Representative Rivers RISES and crosses to the window.*]

JACK Mr. Rivers, I meant to say this before, but I really appreciate you treating us to lunch like this. I don't get to eat out much. My wife and I have hardly left the house since....

RIVERS Oh, don't mention it, Mr. Morgan. It's my pleasure, really.

[*Representative Rivers struggles to open the window. It's stuck shut.*]

RIVERS Doesn't want to budge. It's an old building. All this humidity makes the wood swell up.

[*He tries again. Straining himself, he manages to slightly crack the window open.*]

RIVERS That'll have to do. My goodness.... This is some kind of view! Heck of a city from up high. [*CROSSING BACK AND SITTING*] Anyway, where were we? Whose turn is it to speak?

[*Arthur HOLDS UP the spoon.*]

ARTHUR Mine. But I think Jack was trying to elaborate on something. The trial.... how he felt. He never finished.

[*Arthur holds the spoon out to Jack, who hesitates.*]

JACK Oh, that's all right. I really....

[*Arthur drops the spoon on the table in front of Jack. Jack picks it up.*]

JACK Okay.... Well, I don't know if I.... I just get upset a lot and.... Look, I feel bad for bringing this up, Arthur. Everything you've had to go through.... I mean, it's a nightmare for all of us.

But what happened that day.... Stupid recklessness. An accidental discharge, honest to God. [*to Representative Rivers*] But assault with a deadly weapon? Six years? Jesus! The kid's barely eighteen. And that arm of his.... God, he had such a future. Can't we.... isn't there something that can be done?

RIVERS [*taking the spoon*] Messy process, Mr. Morgan, and I don't think.... But this is good, though! Opening up to each other. That's what we want. [*handing the spoon to Arthur*] Mr. Gilligan?

[*Arthur looks at Jack coldly.*]

ARTHUR I think you should be grateful.

JACK Excuse me?

RIVERS [*warning Jack*] Ah ah ... !

ARTHUR Your boy's healthy, safe. In six years, he'll even be able to get some normalcy back into his life. Be grateful.

JACK You think he's safe in there? Locked up with all them....

[*As he trails off, Arthur leans forward with interest.*]

JACK He can't.... He's not like them. He's not....

RIVERS Mr. Morgan. You don't have the spoon.

ARTHUR So where do you suppose people who put bullets in other people's heads ought to go?

RIVERS Hey now! Let's try to keep things....

JACK I thank God every day that your son's still alive. I can't imagine how hard it must be to.... But you need to know Cliff like I do. He would never have intentionally....

ARTHUR Alive? The only thing Garrett can do on his own is breathe. He can't use the bathroom. He can't move. He can't even respond to his mother's touch. While your son eats warm, solid food, mine gets fed through a tube in his gut! Is that "alive" to you?

RIVERS [*with frustration*] That's enough! Now, I know you two ain't the best of friends, and this is a sensitive issue, but there's no way we're gonna get past it unless we stay on the high road! [*beat*] So. . . . can we do this like men? Huh? Can we?

[*Jack slowly nods at Representative Rivers.*]

RIVERS Mr. Gilligan?

ARTHUR Sure.

RIVERS Good. I knew you two were reasonable. I could smell it. Now, I'm going to ask you both some questions. And I want honesty. [*handing the spoon to Jack*] Mr. Morgan. . . . what do you want from Mr. Gilligan today?

JACK Well. . . . I want him to, you know. . . . to entertain the possibility that my son didn't mean to do what he did. And if I'm right about this, his sentence. . . . it doesn't fit. Don't you think? [*turning to Representative Rivers*] I mean, it wouldn't. . . . Don't you think so?

RIVERS [*taking the spoon*] Perhaps. Mr. Gilligan, wouldn't you say, considering all the uncertainty, that Mr. Morgan might have a point? [*handing the spoon to Arthur*] How can we know for sure this whole thing wasn't accidental?

ARTHUR Outside of the jury's verdict? Twelve people all thinking otherwise? I don't know. . . .

RIVERS [*surprised*] Good. That's good! See, this is progress. This is how we get somewhere. Civil discourse. Now, let's keep going. Mr. Gilligan, what do you want from Mr. Morgan?

ARTHUR I just want a little reciprocation here. [*to Jack*] I want him to "entertain the possibility" that his son did just what he meant to.

JACK Oh, come on now.

RIVERS [*a warning to Jack*] Mr. Morgan. . . .

[*Arthur suddenly TOSSES THE SPOON OVER HIS SHOULDER. Representative Rivers stares back with disbelief.*]

RIVERS What'd you do that for?!

ARTHUR We're done passing fucking spoons around.

RIVERS [*patience wearing thin*] Alright, alright, that's fine. If the spoon's not working for you, then we'll just move on to something....

ARTHUR How about we don't! How about for once, you just sit there and let us talk this out ourselves?

RIVERS Well, I don't.... I don't really, uh.... Alright, I guess, but....

ARTHUR Now listen, Jack. Pam and I.... we've been wondering. Well, before she left me, that is, we were wondering.... why do you think Cliff took out that gun?

[*Jack glares at Arthur uncomfortably, remains silent.*]

ARTHUR I'm waiting.

JACK He was upset.

ARTHUR You mean angry, don't you? Baseball was his life. Isn't that what he said in court? He was angry, Jack.

JACK Angry, upset, whatever! But he never meant to fire the goddamn thing!

[*Representative Rivers begins wiping his brow with a napkin.*]

ARTHUR And how do you know that, exactly? Top shortstop in the state. Colleges drooling all over him. And then my boy has to go and jeopardize it all by threatening to tell Coach he's juicing. He felt betrayed, and he had a gun. How can you be positive he didn't just snap?

JACK Because I was there right after he did it. I heard the bang and ran upstairs. He couldn't believe what he had done. Found him just rocking back and forth in front of his bed. He was in complete disbelief. Kept saying to me, "I killed him, Dad. I killed him...." He was so pale. His face.... that wasn't the face of someone who meant to shoot his best friend!

ARTHUR Oh, I'm sure he was just bawling his eyes out when he grabbed that pistol from the drawer and started waving it in Garrett's face. What's accidental about pointing a gun at someone? If there were true justice in the world, they would've nailed your son for attempted murder!

[*Jack RISES from the table.*]

JACK [*furious*] That's it, you son of a bitch!

RIVERS [*holding Jack back*] Easy, easy!

JACK Do you really believe your family is the only victim here?! We're all suffering! And I don't give a fuck what you think.

ARTHUR Apparently not.

RIVERS Stop! Both of you, stop! [*beat as things settle*] God almighty! What happened to the high road? I thought we'd be able to find some common ground here. I really did. Let me tell you two what's going to happen if you can't work things out. You'll be miserable for the rest of your lives. You'll grow spiteful and bitter. And that void you both feel inside.... that blackness.... it'll grow. And it won't stop growing until you two make amends!

JACK He's too resentful.

ARTHUR You're too deluded.

RIVERS Now, listen here! These quips.... this whole back and forth thing you've got going on.... that's not how God-fearing people discuss things! All I want is for each of you to leave here with some sense of peace. Can't you both....

ARTHUR [*annoyed*] Just shut up! You don't give a shit about us.

[*Representative Rivers is dumbfounded.*]

ARTHUR All you want is publicity. How many pictures did we have to take outside?

RIVERS [*defensively*] I. . . . That. . . . That's untrue! That's just. . . .

ARTHUR I know where you've been aligning yourself. "No" to magazine capacity restrictions. "No" to expanded background checks. You want teachers to bring guns into their classrooms, for God's sake. The story. . . . The trial. . . . damned inconvenient for you.

JACK Christ!

ARTHUR So what better than to bring the two parties together to smooth things over?

RIVERS You're here for one reason. . . . so that you can both move forward with your lives. To say I don't care. . . . that is just. . . . that's upsetting! And I'm not going to tolerate it.

ARTHUR I'm not going to tolerate you, you sweaty piece of shit! You and your concealed carry crusade.

RIVERS [*RISING anxiously*] I thought I could help. But if this is the way I'm going to be spoken to. . . . I'm done. And making this political? Trying to turn it around like I'm just here on some sort of agenda? Now that's petty. You bring up concealed carry laws, but your boy getting shot has got nothing to do with them.

ARTHUR But *this* does.

[*Arthur reaches inside his coat, PULLS OUT A PISTOL. Jack and Representative Rivers go pale.*]

RIVERS [*to Arthur*] Jesus, put that away!

ARTHUR [*to Representative Rivers*] Sit back down.

RIVERS Mr. Gilligan.

ARTHUR I said sit down!

[*Timidly, Representative Rivers returns to his seat. A moment of tense silence passes as the three stare at one another.*]

RIVERS Look.... We're all civilized men here. We can....

ARTHUR You keep throwing that word around like it means something!

JACK Let's just keep calm, alright? There's no need for this to escalate. Now, why'd you go and bring that in here?

ARTHUR BECAUSE NO ONE'S LISTENING, GODDAMN IT! Not the lawyers. Not the judge. Not the media. [*pointing the gun at Representative Rivers*] Not him! [*pointing it at Jack*] And not you! But now you have to listen! And I'm telling you.... six years is a joke for what your son did.

JACK [*slouching away from the gun*] I know it seems that way, but Cliff.... he wouldn't have pulled that trigger on purpose. Arthur, you've known him for years. He's a good kid who just made a horrible mistake.

RIVERS [*attempting to keep things calm*] Mr. Morgan, how about we just not argue right now.

ARTHUR You're not trying to convince me, Jack. You're not even trying to convince Mr. Second Amendment here. You're just trying to convince yourself because you can't face the fact that your boy would do such a thing.

JACK Arthur, put down the gun.

[*Arthur keeps the gun raised, his hands shaking in anger.*]

JACK Arthur, you put that gun down right now!

ARTHUR Why?

JACK Because you're in no state to be holding it!

ARTHUR Why not?

JACK [*with intensity*] Because you're all heated up! You're out of control! You're. . . .

[*Upon realizing what he's said, Jack's eyes suddenly widen and his gaze drops away. Arthur notices this shift in demeanor. After a moment, TEARS begin to drip down Jack's face. Soon he's CRYING. Arthur continues staring as Jack begins to SOB IN EARNEST. Arthur's fierce expression gradually morphs into somberness as he watches Jack break down in front of him. He eases his grip on the pistol and with dismal eyes, lowers the gun back onto the table and lightly shoves it forward. As the gun comes to a rest in the center of the table, Representative Rivers RISES with a deep, relieved sigh.*]

RIVERS Jesus!

[*Representative Rivers CROSSES back to the window, takes a few long breaths, then turns back to Arthur and Jack. He gazes bleakly at them for a moment, then shakes his head and leans against the windowsill. Arthur leans back in his chair and sighs. His success has left him uncomfortable and unsure as to what he's accomplished. He picks up an empty glass from the table. After fiddling with it for a while, he lethargically puts it back down and rubs his forehead.*]

JACK [*weary*] Where's that damn waitress?

[*The three men remain locked into their respective experiences as the LIGHTS . . .*]

FADE TO BLACK

END OF PLAY

The Sixth Chamber

BY ADAM ROPER

Copyright © by Adam Roper. All rights reserved. Published with permission from the author. Inquiries concerning rights should be addressed to Adam Roper at aroper20@gmail.com.

The Sixth Chamber

Premiered November 15, 2012 | Swain Hall, Studio 6 Theatre, UNC Department of Communication | Directed by Dana Marks

CHARACTERS

Original cast members are in brackets.

GUS   30s, male. The owner of a club [Trevor Johnson].

NICOLE   30s, female. Gus's girlfriend/helper [Laurel Ullman].

HERM   30s, male. Nicole's ex-husband [Keegan Cotton].

TIME & SETTING

Present. Gus' club, Herm's apartment.

SCENE ONE

LIGHTS UP

On a SEEDY CLUB after hours. GUS sits at the bar, counting a stack of money. A REVOLVER rests nearby. NICOLE MOPS the floor. Gus glances over at her.

GUS   Come on, baby, you missed some by the chair there. Don't get sloppy on me now, or I might not get you that necklace you've been eyeing.

NICOLE   This isn't my first time cleaning up after one of your games, Gus.

[*Nicole continues to mop when suddenly the DOOR KICKS OPEN. Gus reaches for the revolver as HERM enters with confidence. Nicole, surprised, stops mopping.*]

GUS Bar's closed, so you best turn right around and.... Wait a second, is that? Hot damn! It is, ole Herm. What're you doing, busting in like that, big guy?

HERM I'm here for Nicole.

GUS [*chuckling*] That right? You kill me, boy. Get outta here.

HERM I came for my wife, Gus, and I'm not leaving without her.

GUS Oh, really? Come on, buddy, out!

NICOLE Leave, Herm. Please!

HERM [*to Gus*] Stand up and fight me.

GUS Nah, I'm not going to embarrass you again, champ. Listen to Nicole.

HERM [*noticing the revolver*] I'll play you for her, then. Whoever wins gets my wife.

GUS You're just full of 'em today, aren't you?

[*Herm CROSSES to a table, picks up a rag, wipes blood off the seat, SITS, then gestures for Gus to join him.*]

GUS You serious?

[*Herm holds firm. Gus looks over at Nicole, who stares back anxiously.*]

HERM What's the matter? Let me guess. You don't actually play, do you? You just set up the games and take your cut, right? You too scared, Gus?

NICOLE Herm!

GUS No, it's okay. I got this. So you want to play with the big boys, huh?

[*Gus opens the cylinder to his revolver and DUMPS OUT FIVE BULLETS. He then spins the chamber, places it in the middle of the table, and SITS across from Herm.*]

GUS You might want to think long and hard about this, now. Don't want to do something you'll end up regretting.

[*After a beat, Herm SPINS THE REVOLVER and watches as it slowly STOPS with the barrel POINTING AT GUS. Herm SLIDES IT over to Gus, who pauses for a moment, nods, then picks it up.*]

NICOLE Gus, don't do this.

[*Gus puts the revolver to his head and PULLS THE TRIGGER. Nicole GASPS. It CLICKS. Smiling, he SLIDES IT BACK OVER TO HERM, who solemnly picks it up.*]

NICOLE Herm, what do you think you're doing?

HERM Saving you.

[*Herm PUTS THE REVOLVER TO HIS HEAD.*]

END OF SCENE

SCENE TWO

[*HERM'S APARTMENT. Herm sadly SHUFFLES IN, closes the door behind him and PLOPS onto the couch with a sigh.*]

NICOLE [*offstage*] Herm?

HERM In here.

[*Nicole ENTERS from another room.*]

NICOLE What're you doing home so early? I thought you were working another party tonight.

HERM Chuck let me go. Said I wasn't "superhero material."

NICOLE Oh, Herm!

HERM It's fine, I'll find something else. For now, though, I just want to relax with my wife.

[*A COUGH from offstage.*]

HERM Someone here?

[*Gus ENTERS from the other room, buttoning up his shirt.*]

GUS Oh, Hey. You must be Herm. The name's Gus. Nice to actually meet you.

[*Gus extends his hand for a shake. Herm ignores the gesture.*]

HERM Aren't you the guy from the bar who . . . ?

GUS I apologize for that. I never should have grabbed Nicky with you right there and all.

HERM [*to Nicole*] Are you and him . . . ?

GUS Afraid so, big guy.

NICOLE I'm so sorry, Herm. I never meant to hurt you. I just. . . . I'm leaving with Gus.

GUS It's nothing personal, now. Nicole here just needs more of a. . . . well, a man. You know how women are.

[*Herm suddenly PUNCHES Gus in the chest. Gus, unfazed, takes Nicole's arm and leads her toward the door. Nicole looks back at Herm sympathetically before they both EXIT.*]

END OF SCENE

SCENE THREE

[*THE CLUB. We pick up at the end of the last scene, with Herm holding the revolver to his head. Herm PULLS THE TRIGGER. IT CLICKS. He calmly places it back down on the table.*]

NICOLE [*beside herself*] Jesus, will you two stop?!

GUS Well, would you look at that?

[*Herm stares Gus down as he SLIDES THE REVOLVER OVER TO HIM AGAIN.*]

GUS   You really want to keep going, buddy?

[*Herm maintains eye contact.*]

GUS   [*picking up the gun*] Well, alright then.

NICOLE   That's it, I'm done.

[*Nicole drops the mop and begins to exit. Both men quickly RISE.*]

HERM   Nicky, wait!

NICOLE   I'm not going to sit here and watch this. It's crazy.

[*Gus CROSSES to Nicole and takes her aside.*]

GUS   [*discreetly*] Listen, baby, you know I love you, right? Trust me, I have this under control.

[*Nicole sighs and CROSSES back into the room. Gus takes his seat, gun in hand. Herm gestures for him to continue. GUS PUTS THE REVOLVER TO HIS HEAD. Nicole winces and turns her head away. GUS PULLS THE TRIGGER. CLICK. He calmly places it back down. Herm stares at it for a long moment.*]

GUS   We can call it here, Herm. Both of us can walk away right now. You just promise to leave us alone.

[*Herm picks up the revolver.*]

NICOLE   Herm!

HERM   [*to Nicole*] Come back with me. You shouldn't be with him.

[*Herm RISES and APPROACHES her.*]

HERM   This isn't what you want.

[*Gus quickly stands in between the two.*]

GUS You stay away from her with that. This is between you and me.

HERM What? I would never. . . .

[*Gus stares him down. Herm sighs sadly. His eyes fall to the revolver. Slowly, he PUTS IT TO HIS HEAD.*]

END OF SCENE

SCENE FOUR

[*HERM'S APARTMENT. Herm holds onto Nicole for support as they ENTER.*]

NICOLE Come on, sit down.

HERM I almost had him, Nicky. I really did.

NICOLE Why are you even getting into bar fights? That guy was twice your size.

HERM I'm okay. Really. Look, I'm sorry.

NICOLE It's fine.

HERM No, it's not. You always tell me I shouldn't be doing this kind of thing.

NICOLE Then why do you?

HERM I'm not just going to let someone disrespect my fiancée like that. Plus, I'm a superhero, remember. . . . it's my job to protect women in distress.

NICOLE You play dress-up for parties, Herm. Besides, all he did was grab my ass. Trust me, I've had a lot worse done to me.

HERM Well, you don't deserve that.

NICOLE It's not worth you getting your head kicked in. I appreciate what you're trying to do, but that's just how guys are. I've learned to deal with it. You don't need to protect me.

HERM   I want to, though. I love you, Nicky. I don't want to see anything happen to you.

NICOLE   I'm sorry. It's just. . . . I love you too, I do. More than you probably know. But I can't stand seeing you hurt like this. And I feel like it's my fault. If it weren't for me, this never would've happened.

HERM   Well, don't. You're worth it.

[*Nicole gives him a half-smile, touches his hand gently, but looks away with concern.*]

END OF SCENE

SCENE FIVE

[*THE CLUB. We pick up at the end of the last scene, with Herm holding the revolver to his head. As Gus and Nicole watch anxiously, HE PULLS THE TRIGGER. CLICK. With a small sigh, he places it on the table.*]

GUS   [*suddenly nervous*] Alright, buddy. You proved your point. Let's call this.

HERM   Something wrong, Gus?

[*Herm SLIDES THE REVOLVER across the table, and gives him a look that says, "Go ahead." Gus doesn't move.*]

HERM   You don't know which chamber the round's in. . . . fifth or sixth. Am I right?

GUS   That's the point of the game.

HERM   Unless you're able to spin it so the bullet is always in one of those two chambers. [*beat*] You never thought I'd make it this far, did you? [*beat*] I'm going to take my wife back now.

GUS   As soon as one of us is dead.

HERM   After you.

[*In a prideful rage, Gus quickly grabs the revolver. Nicole SCREAMS. But Gus PUTS IT TO HIS HEAD AND PULLS THE TRIGGER.... CLICK. Gus falls into his chair with relief and lays the gun down. Herm stares at it for a moment, THEN REACHES FOR IT.*]

NICOLE Don't be crazy!

GUS Slow down there, cowboy. We're ending it here.

HERM [*to Nicky*] Just come with me.

[*Nicole looks away ashamed. Gus puts his arm around her protectively.*]

NICOLE I'm sorry, Herm. [*beat*] But, I can't be saved.

[*Herm lets out a small, defeated LAUGH. After a long pause, he reaches out, PICKS UP THE REVOLVER, AND PUTS IT TO HIS TEMPLE.*]

END OF SCENE

SCENE SIX

[*HERM'S APARTMENT. Herm sits on his couch wearing a cheap-looking BATMAN COSTUME AND MASK. He's staring at a GUN in his hand. Slowly, HE PUTS THE GUN TO HIS MOUTH AND COCKS IT. Suddenly, there's a KNOCK on the door. Herm HIDES THE GUN, RISES, CROSSES to the door, and OPENS IT, revealing Nicole. She has a BLACK EYE.*]

NICOLE [*noticing the costume*] Oh!

[*Herm, off her reaction, quickly pulls off the mask.*]

HERM Sorry, it's for work.

NICOLE I don't mean to bother you. I'm Nicole; I live a few doors down.

HERM Herm. Nice to meet you.

[*Herm extends his hand. Nicole looks at it cautiously.*]

NICOLE I just wanted to apologize about all the noise earlier. My ex-boyfriend Gus was moving out, and. . . .

HERM Oh, I'm sorry to hear that. I've seen you two around. [*beat*] Did he do that to your eye?

NICOLE I just wanted to apologize about the noise. I'm sorry to bother you.

[*She turns to leave.*]

HERM Wait, let me take care of that for you. I've got an ice pack in the freezer.

[*She hesitates.*]

HERM Please.

[*With a small smile, she relents and ENTERS. Herm EXITS to another room as Nicole takes a seat on the couch.*]

NICOLE [*calling off*] So what exactly do you do for a living?

HERM [*offstage*] You mean, why am I dressed as Batman?

NICOLE [*laughing*] Yeah.

HERM [*offstage*] It's for a party rental company. I dress up as different superheroes for kids' birthday parties or events and stuff.

[*Herm RE-ENTERS holding an ICE PACK and heads for the couch.*]

HERM It's kind of stupid, and I don't fill it out very well.

NICOLE I don't know; there's nothing sexier than a man in uniform.

[*Both LAUGH nervously, the tension breaking.*]

HERM Yeah, no, I'm actually not supposed to take the costume home. I'm sure I'll hear about it tomorrow from Chuck.

NICOLE Why'd you do it then?

[*Long beat as his eyes dart to the place where he hid the gun. Then returning his gaze to Nicole....*]

HERM Here.

[*He gently puts the ice pack on her eye. She leans back into his arm.*]

NICOLE That feels good. [*long beat*] My hero.

[*Herm smiles broadly.*]

FADE TO BLACK

END OF PLAY

Bad Connection

BY RACHEL SCHMITT

Copyright © by Rachel Schmitt. All rights reserved. Published with permission from the author. Inquiries concerning rights should be addressed to Rachel Schmitt at rmschmitt13@gmail.com.

Bad Connection

Presented October 23, 2015 | Kenan Theatre, UNC Department of Dramatic Art | Directed by Dana Coen

CHARACTERS

Original cast members are in brackets.

NARRATOR 20, female. She stands at the back of the party and eats all the guacamole. Insightful and sassy [Kat Froehlich].

EMMA 20, female. She's intelligent, makes fun of people who spend all their time on their phones, even though she does it as well [Claire Koenig].

WES 21, male. A stereotypical rom-com hot trope with a secret sensitive side, very aware of his good looks; over all a pretty decent guy [Byron Frazelle].

AMY 21, female. She's incredibly driven, tech savvy, very sure of herself, shallow [Mackenzie Kwok].

JEREMY 20, male. He's a jerk, but to be honest that's kind of his charm; pretty clueless when it comes to reading other people's feelings [Jerome Allen].

FRAT BRO 19, male. Drunk and passed out [James Scalise].

TIME & SETTING

Present. The front porch at a college house party.

LIGHTS UP

On the front porch of a house. DANCE MUSIC can be heard from inside. The NARRATOR stands off next to a table on top of which is a large bowl of guacamole. She holds an open bag of chips. A FRAT BRO is PASSED OUT underneath the table. Downstage, EMMA and WES sit on opposite sides of a ratty couch, completely absorbed with their PHONES.

NARRATOR [to the audience] It's a Saturday night, and here we are with fifty-six of our closest friends at the house party of that girl your roommate's friend knows from his poli class. There's a weird smell wafting from the bathroom and, like, no furniture in the entire house.... unless you count a ratty couch, covered in PJ stains of parties past and pet throw-up from that one time the house cat got sick and no one bothered to clean it up for a week because it was midterms.... but mostly because college students are disgusting.

[She DIPS A CHIP in the guacamole and takes a crunchy bite.]

NARRATOR [to the audience, re: Emma] This is Emma, intelligent, driven, and the proud owner of a semi-popular Tumblr blog. That's Wes, who looks like he walked straight out of a J.Crew® catalog. He's sensitive and kind of self-righteous, but not in a way that keeps you from thinking he's hot.

[Emma TAKES PHOTOS of herself with her phone. Wes LAUGHS at something the audience can't see on his screen.]

NARRATOR [to the audience] Emma is busy trying to get the right ugly-to-cute ratio for her Snapchat pictures. Wes is laughing at a YouTube video. It's probably about cats. You'd think after sitting out here for forty-five minutes together they'd have struck up a conversation, but that would require some social intelligence, so instead they're just going to pretend like they don't see each other.

[*A PHONE RINGS. Emma and Wes both check to see if it belongs to them. Wes RISES to answer it. Emma returns to her phone. Throughout Wes's conversation, Emma periodically reacts to unseen texts.*]

WES Amy? Amy? Can you. . . . can you hear me? Where are you? I looked everywhere. [*beat*] I'm out on the porch. [*beat*] It was too hot inside, and it's a lot more chill out here. I mean, there's a guy passed out, but I'm like eighty-seven percent sure he's not dead. . . . Left? Of course I haven't left. I'm seriously out on the porch right now. [*becoming increasingly frustrated*] Damn it, Amy! I'm still at the party! [*beat*] Wait. . . . what did you just call me? Amy? Amy, are you even listening?

[*AMY ENTERS, checks her phone.*]

NARRATOR This is Amy, Wes's girlfriend. She's social media obsessed, always has a perfect profile pic, and probably knows what quinoa is.

AMY [*noticing Wes*] Baby! There you are! You are not even going to guess what I just saw! I was walking down the hall and talking to you on the phone, remember that? So anyways. . . .

WES I'm confused.

AMY How can you be confused? I literally just started the story. I'll start over. So I was walking down the hall. . . .

WES No, Amy. I'm not confused about your story. Weren't we just in the middle of a fight?

[*Amy looks at him, puzzled.*]

WES You thought I'd left? You called me names I haven't heard since fourth grade that may or may not still have the ability to hurt my feelings? Is any of this ringing a bell?

AMY I've moved on. I'm trying to tell you a hysterical story, so are you going to listen or not? [*not waiting for a reply*] So anyway, I was on the phone with you and walking down the hall and then I saw Lizzie Larabee. You know, the transfer from Texas? [*beat*] Anyway, she's drunk out of her mind.

[*Amy searches her phone for a video, finds it, then hands the phone to Wes.*]

AMY Wait, see.... she's about to jump on the table.

WES That's an interesting move she's doing there.

NARRATOR [*to the audience*] An interpretive dance to R. Kelly's "Ignition."

AMY Oh my God, this is amazing. She's so going to regret this in the morning. [*taking the phone back from him*] What's a good hashtag to put with this?

WES You're not actually going to post this, right? That could get her in serious trouble. Her parents could see it, or potential employers. She could lose her scholarship.

AMY God, thank you, Hermione Granger from Harry Potter books one through five. I'm not an idiot. I'm posting it to Twitter, not Facebook. Everyone knows old people don't go on Twitter unless they're a business owner trying to "get down" with the youth.

[*A TEXT TONE is heard. Amy, Wes, and Emma all check their phones. It's for Amy.*]

AMY I've gotta go. Mikayla's ex has been sub-tweeting her all night, so I need to be with her.

[*Amy RUNS OFF. Wes sits back on the couch and returns to his phone. Emma and Wes gaze at their phones in silence. After a moment, Emma looks up at Wes for the first time. At the moment she chooses to speak, JEREMY ENTERS from stage left.*]

NARRATOR [*to the audience*] Enter Jeremy, Emma's on-again, off-again boyfriend. He's a bit of a jerk, but the part of me who roots for Kanye West and post-Esquire-interview Miles Teller is kind of into it.

[*Jeremy sits between Emma and Wes on the couch.*]

JEREMY Hey, boo.

EMMA   Jeremy, where have you even been all night? I've been bored out of my mind, and a girl can only pretend to text for so long.

JEREMY   Sorry, I've been out socializing with the locals.

EMMA   I've been wanting to talk to you about something. . . .

JEREMY   Wait. Before we get into this, we're together now, right?

EMMA   I'm going to choose to believe that you're asking this as a joke.

JEREMY   Just wanted to make sure everything was cool since I accidentally matched with your friend on Tinder.

EMMA   Jeremy, I need you to take our relationship more. . . . wait, you did what?

JEREMY   In my defense, I didn't realize you had hot friends.

EMMA   Can you pay attention for one minute? You know how I've been applying for internships, and how I told you the other day that I got an interview with a firm up in New York City?

JEREMY   [*unaware*] Yes. . . .

EMMA   Anyway, they offered me the job.

[*Emma pauses, waiting for a reply, but Jeremy is too busy taking a selfie of them.*]

EMMA   Are you even listening to me?

NARRATOR   [*to the audience*] He is not.

EMMA   I honestly can't even believe you right now. I'm trying to have a serious conversation because I'm trying to decide whether I should travel to a big city I've never been to for a barely paid internship, or stay at home and earn some savings, but you're too busy being a total. . . . [*noticing the photo*] wait, we actually look pretty cute in that pic. [*then shifting back*] No! No! I'm mad at you! [*recovering her composure*] I really need some advice. What do you think I should do?

NARRATOR [*to the audience*] Wait for it. . . .

JEREMY [*not looking up from his phone*] About what?

[*Upset, Emma groans, RISES, and STORMS OFFSTAGE.*]

[*A TEXT TONE CHIMES. Both Wes and Jeremy check their phones. It's for Jeremy.*]

JEREMY Solid. Another match. [*to Wes*] You got Tinder, man?

WES I've got a girlfriend.

JEREMY Yeah well, so do I, but who am I to deny the ladies the chance to check all this out.

[*Jeremy continues to play with his phone. He leans over to show Wes his phone screen.*]

JEREMY Swipe right, or nah?

[*Before Wes can respond. . . .*]

AMY [*calling from offstage*] Baby!

WES Crap! [*to Jeremy*] Pretend I wasn't here.

[*Wes heads for the door, BUMPING INTO EMMA as she ENTERS. They look at each other with interest, but soon awkwardly turn away. Amy ENTERS, searching for Wes, shrugs, CROSSES to the couch and SITS. Emma takes a seat between Amy and Jeremy, ignoring the latter.*]

JEREMY Come on, Emma! You can't just ignore me like a three a.m. fire drill.

[*Emma turns her back to him. He returns to his phone and CROSSES AWAY.*]

AMY [*to Emma*] Boyfriend trouble?

EMMA It's complicated.

AMY *It's Complicated* is a movie title, not a relationship status.

EMMA   That's actually pretty good. Did you come up with that?

AMY   I read that on a T-shirt at Forever 21 once, but that doesn't make it any less true.

[*There is an awkward pause.*]

EMMA   So, do you know Molly, the host?

AMY   Not really, but I do follow her on Twitter. Which, B-T-dubs, is kind of a big deal because I don't really follow a lot of people. I try to keep my feed clean, you know? And besides, I can't be following more people than I have followers. Social suicide. But it's, like, not a problem for me. I'm kind of semi-Twitter famous.

NARRATOR   [*to the audience*] Did anyone else follow that? Because I think I blacked out for a moment.

EMMA   Semi-Twitter famous?

AMY   I do a lot of commentary on the present-day iPhone, emoji climate. . . . uses, meanings, and what's missing from the current collection.

[*Emma is growing disinterested.*]

AMY   It's not always easy or fun, but someone has to do it. There's a BuzzFeed article about it. You probably saw it.

[*Emma looks at her wrist as if she were wearing a watch.*]

EMMA   Oh my gosh! I just realized that I promised to meet my friend in another room of the party at exactly this time!

AMY   Totally cool! Talk later.

[*Emma EXITS just as Wes ENTERS. They again make eye contact. Amy spots Wes, breaks the moment.*]

AMY   Oh, how nice of you to join me.

[*Wes joins Amy on the couch. Jeremy stands off quietly taking selfies.*]

WES Amy, I've been doing some thinking. And I've also been doing some drinking, and I've come to the conclusion that this just isn't working.

AMY What? Us? How could you even say that?

WES Come on. You only date me because I look good in Instagram photos.

AMY You do look flawless in every filter.

WES But is that a reason to keep dating?

AMY You're saying I'm only dating you because you're attractive? I have guys hitting me up on my social media profiles left and right. Even on LinkedIn!

WES I just can't do this. I need someone who's going to take the time to listen to what I. . . .

AMY [*interrupting*] I know what this is really about! You're just jealous that Apple reached out to me about my analysis of their emojis. If I learned anything from Beyoncé's performance at the two thousand fourteen VMAs, it's that I don't need a guy who feels threatened by my success.

WES Yeah, well, I don't need a woman who objectifies me.

[*Amy, gazing at her phone, RISES and CROSSES AWAY.*]

WES Amy! Are you even listening?

[*She EXITS. Wes sighs and takes a seat on the couch. Emma ENTERS. Jeremy INTERCEPTS.*]

JEREMY Hey babe, I'm sorry you got mad at me for, like, no reason, but I'm ready to forgive you. I'm pretty sure there's a closet out in the hallway with a minimal amount of puke. Want to go there and make out?

EMMA You're actually super disgusting. Do you even know why I'm mad at you?

JEREMY [*flipping through his phone*] Uh, of course. You got mad because your parents won't let you go to that internship you want in L.A.

EMMA That's it. I'm done. We're done.

JEREMY Please. You've said that before.

EMMA Well, this time I mean it. You never listen to me when I talk to you! We just need to stop whatever it is we have going on here.

JEREMY Well, don't expect me to like your Instagram pics anymore.

[*Jeremy EXITS. Emma takes a seat on the couch next to Wes.*]

WES [*turning to her*] You should do it.

EMMA Sorry?

WES The internship, I mean. It'll be scary and maybe you'll have to start getting creative with ramen, but I think it would be worth it.

EMMA You were listening to that?

WES Umm, yeah. I hope that's okay and not at all creepy.

EMMA [*laughing*] No, it's just that. . . . I never think *anyone's* ever listening. . . .

[*Emma and Wes gaze at each other before shyly turning away. Then. . . .*]

EMMA You really think I should do it? Maybe I should just stay home and earn some extra cash.

WES Or you could accept an awesome internship in New York, and then, in your free time, walk around the city and recreate scenes from *Ghostbusters*.

[*She grins, blushes. He returns the smile.*]

NARRATOR [*to the audience*] They're so freaking cute. I just want to rip out my eyes but then put them back in so I can keep watching.

EMMA You know what, I think I'm going to do it. I really want to, and now I feel like it'll be a personal affront to Bill Murray if I don't.

WES That's the spirit! Can I grab you a drink.... to celebrate?

EMMA Definitely!

[*Wes RISES. After a brief moment, Emma follows suit.*]

EMMA You know what? I'll go with you.

WES I'm Wes.

EMMA Emma.

[*They again exchange smiles, POCKET THEIR PHONES, and EXIT together.*]

NARRATOR [*to the audience*] This is so stupid romantic. Look at them, riding off into the sunset with the promise of a beautiful relationship and maybe some making out later. [*beat*] Maybe there's hope for us yet.

[*A TEXT TONE RINGS OUT from INSIDE THE GUACAMOLE BOWL. The FRAT BRO awakens and RISES unsteadily from beneath the table. He looks around for a moment before reaching into the guacamole bowl and PULLING OUT A PHONE. The Narrator looks on in horror.*]

FRAT BRO I knew I left this somewhere.

[*He wipes the guacamole off the phone and begins TEXTING as he EXITS. The Narrator stares out into the audience in defeat.*]

LIGHTS FADE OUT

END OF PLAY

Vinegar Syndrome

BY RACHEL SHOPE

Copyright © by Rachel Shope. All rights reserved. Published with permission from the author. Inquiries concerning rights should be addressed to Rachel Shope at racheleshope@gmail.com.

Vinegar Syndrome

Premiered November 15, 2012 | Swain Hall, Studio 6 Theatre, UNC Department of Communication | Directed by Joseph Megel

CHARACTERS

Original cast members are in brackets.

VIRGIL 20s, male. A romantic leading man in an old, colorized movie [Keith Gavigan].

AGNES 20s, female. A romantic ingénue in an old, colorized movie [Ashley Lucas].

PIM 20s, female. A film restoration expert [Page Purgar].

GARY 20s, male. Pim's husband [Doug Pass].

TIME & SETTING

Present. A film restoration lab.

LIGHTS UP

On a studio in a film restoration lab. PIM is slouched over a computer, typing furiously. She pauses a moment to yawn, then presses the "play" button. On the "PROJECTION SCREEN," which is actually a life-sized FRAME for the actors, VIRGIL, the dashing leading man, and AGNES, the demure heroine, are in the midst of a scene.

VIRGIL Speak in earnest now, Agnes; [*almost inaudible*] can you promise me your whole self?

[*Pim furrows her brow and clicks a button, causing Agnes and Virgil to FREEZE. She types and clicks, then REWINDS until they are in their original positions and clicks "play."*]

VIRGIL [*speaking at normal volume*] Can you promise me your whole self? [*pulling Agnes close*] Tell me the truth, darling! I won't settle for anything less.

AGNES But Virgil, that is nothing I have to promise. . . . that is truth itself! Dearest, I am no self at all without you.

[*They lean toward each other for a kiss. There is a KNOCK on the studio door. Pim FREEZES THE IMAGE, just before their lips touch.*]

GARY [*offstage*] Pim?

PIM Yeah?

[*Pim's husband, GARY, ENTERS. He is dressed in khakis and a button-down shirt.*]

GARY Hey, babe. [*kissing her on the cheek*] You ready?

PIM Oh my God! I completely lost track of time. Can you wait a few more minutes? It's not quite done yet. They don't play until eight, right?

GARY Yeah, but I made dinner reservations at The Delilah at six thirty.

PIM What time is it now?

GARY Six ten.

PIM That's perfect! I can be done in ten minutes, and that'll give us time to drive over there. I'll change in the car.

GARY You're pushin' it, m'lady. What're you working on?

PIM *Virgil*.

GARY Big bad network premiere's still breathing down your pretty neck?

PIM The film was starting to decay.

GARY Is that why it reeks of vinegar in here?

PIM Yes, and that's why it's taking me so long. And the longer we keep chatting, the longer I have to stay.

GARY Alright, alright, I'll wait outside. I can't stand that smell, anyway.

[*He kisses her and EXITS.*]

PIM [*yelling off*] I'll be there in a sec!

[*Pim fiddles with the computer. Virgil and Agnes COMPLETE THEIR KISS. Pim yawns again, REWINDS.*]

AGNES Dearest, I am no self at all without you.

[*Virgil kisses her again. PIM REWINDS.*]

AGNES Dearest, I am no self at all without you.

[*Another kiss. Pim's sleepy eyes droop as she LEANS ON "REWIND."*]

AGNES No self at all without you.

[*Pim lays her head down, causing the film to REWIND YET AGAIN.*]

AGNES Without you.

[*Virgil leans in. This time Agnes STOPS HIM.*]

AGNES Oh, for Heaven's sake, enough!

VIRGIL Agnes! What are you doing?

AGNES What I've wanted to do for the past seventy years!

[*Pim is SNORING. Agnes STOMPS over to the edge of the screen.*]

AGNES You, there! Pim!

[*Pim JOLTS AWAKE, begins CLICKING the "REWIND" BUTTON, which causes Agnes and Virgil to move spastically.*]

AGNES Are you listening to me? I said I've had enough!

[*Pim, trying to concentrate, CLICKS with more intensity. Agnes and Virgil begin JERKING FRANTICALLY.*]

VIRGIL Dear lady, please!

AGNES This is the most exciting thing that's happened in decades.

VIRGIL Oh, Agnes, hush up.

AGNES "Hush up"? Honestly, Virgil! Is that the best you can do? I'm insulted!

PIM [*confused*] Wait, wait. . . .

VIRGIL Insulted? Why ever should you be insulted?

PIM [*a little louder*] I'm sorry, but. . . .

AGNES I'm insulted that anyone would believe that I would fall in love with someone so, so. . . .

VIRGIL So *what*?

AGNES FLAT!

PIM [*exploding*] SHUT UP!

[*Agnes and Virgil BECOME SILENT. Pim RISES and slowly approaches the screen. When her face is close, AGNES MAKES A FACE and JUMPS AT HER, causing Pim to SCREAM.*]

PIM What the hell is going on?!

VIRGIL [*to Agnes*] You've frightened her. [*to Pim*] Terribly sorry for Agnes's wicked actions! Allow me to introduce myself. My name is Vir. . . .

AGNES She knows who we are! She's been cooped up in here gawking at us for weeks.

PIM If this is a joke, it's not funny.

VIRGIL It is not our intention to joke, my dear.

AGNES And even if it was, Virgil's wit is about as sharp as this tacky color scheme you slapped onto us.

PIM What's wrong with the color scheme? I worked hard on that. It's the best it can possibly be, considering the state the film was in when I got my hands on it.

AGNES You should have let it turn to dust.

VIRGIL Agnes, really! There's no need to be cantankerous.

AGNES "Cantankerous"? I've never heard you use so many syllables in one word.

PIM This is ridiculous. The network premiere is a week away and millions of people are going to be watching.

AGNES Millions? I won't have millions of romantic saps getting teary-eyed over this saccharine rubbish. . . . not again.

PIM It's not rubbish. There's a reason why so many want to watch it.

AGNES I find it extremely disheartening that there are that many with such abhorrent taste. If I have to keep pretending to be in love with this. . . . this vapid stereotype, I'll lose my mind!

[*Gary ENTERS. Virgil and Agnes return to the script.*]

VIRGIL [*to Agnes*] Can you promise me your whole self?

GARY Pim, we've got to get going. They'll give our table away if we're late.

VIRGIL [*to Agnes*] Tell me the truth, darling!

PIM Gary, I promise, I am going as fast as I can, okay? But you can't just barge in here. This is my space. You need to knock.

GARY I'm sorry. I know you're working, but Jesus, look at you! You've been putting in crazy hours for the past month and a half. You can call it quits a few minutes early on one special night.

AGNES [*to Virgil*] That is truth itself! Dearest, I.... [*forcing herself to say the words*] am.... no.... self.... at all.... without.... you.

[*This time, they kiss quickly.*]

PIM Five minutes. [*pushing Gary out the door*] That's all I need, I swear.

GARY Pim....

PIM [*closing the door*] Love you! See you soon!

AGNES [*to Pim*] You are a cruel young woman. [*to Virgil*] And you taste like vinegar.

PIM Agnes, I am begging you. Please don't....

AGNES Please don't what, Pim? Do you know what you're begging me to do? Have you ever had to recite the same words over and over again for decades? And they aren't even your words, but you have to say them. And Virgil? Virgil could be any man.... I would still have to say the same words.

PIM But they're lovely words! Nobody says things like that in real life.

AGNES Haven't you ever wondered why that is? I refuse to be part of this dusty charade any longer.

VIRGIL [*grabbing her*] Agnes, for goodness sake! You're not speaking reason! Look at me. Haven't you ever loved me? What about our past? Doesn't it mean anything to you?

[*Agnes starts to swoon, but shakes it off and pushes him away.*]

AGNES What past, Virgil? We have no past! Can you tell me what happened before the first scene? I'll say you can't, because nothing happened. There's only this loop; these god-awful, sleep-inducing, ninety measly minutes.... FOREVER!

PIM [*to Agnes*] Do you have any idea what most people would give to not have to drag their pasts around all the time and just live in the moment? There's no script out here. It's just raw, live-streaming footage, and it's hard. How would you like *that* forever?

VIRGIL You see, Agnes? It's better for us this way, darling.

AGNES [*turns toward him, then away*] Oh, but it isn't enough! I need something more, something.... else.

VIRGIL There is nothing else.

[*A KNOCK on the door.*]

GARY [*offstage*] Pim!

AGNES I need some time alone.

PIM What do you mean, "alone"? [*Agnes walks OFFSCREEN.*] Where are you going? Come back!

GARY [*BARGING IN*] Pim. We have to go. Now!

PIM Jesus, Gary. Look, just go without me. I'll head over there when I finish.

GARY And when will that be? You said you were almost done.

PIM Yeah, well, that was before the leading lady decided she didn't want to be the leading lady anymore.

GARY What's that supposed to mean?

PIM It means that I have to stay here. Because if Agnes and Virgil aren't in love, there is no movie, and if there is no movie, there is no....

GARY You're being ridiculous.

PIM My work is ridiculous to you?

GARY At this moment in time, yes. Come on, get your stuff.

PIM Oh, that's romantic. "Get your stuff." How sweet of you, babe.

GARY Actually, I think you've already killed this evening's romance.

PIM Then what's the point in even going? All the more reason for me to stay here! I'll spend my evening with Virgil!

GARY [*hurt beat*] I hope that works out for you. Just remember that he's not going to follow you home. Happy anniversary.

[*Gary extracts CONCERT TICKETS from his pocket, DROPS THEM ON THE FLOOR, and EXITS. Pim picks them up, looks at them sadly. Then, looking up at the screen....*]

PIM [*to Virgil*] Where did Agnes go?

VIRGIL I expect she ran off to the library scene. It's the only one in which she's alone. It's also the shortest scene in the entire film.

PIM So she should be back soon?

VIRGIL I suppose. And what about Gary? He, too, has run away?

PIM I guess he's going home. [*sullen beat*] It's our anniversary.

VIRGIL Yes, so I hear. If I may, dear Pim.... what are you still doing here?

PIM Well, I can't leave *you* alone.

VIRGIL I think perhaps you and I are not so different from one another, my dear Pim. You understand me.

PIM We've spent quite a bit of time together over the last several weeks. I'm not sorry for that.

VIRGIL Oh, Pim, darling, be my leading lady! Think of it, Pim! Wouldn't it be grand? You and me, together. I would glance at you longingly from afar in the opening scene. You would fall desperately in love with me when I rescue your kitten from the tree in the apple orchard.

PIM   And you could call on me late at night and we'd go swimming in the lake in the dark. . . .

VIRGIL   Yes! And at the end, we would pledge our undying love for each other.

PIM   Yes. . . . and after that?

VIRGIL   Beg pardon?

PIM   What happens after that? After we, you know, pledge our undying love?

VIRGIL   Why, my dear, that's the best part! We go back to the beginning and do it all over again!

PIM   [*Reflecting, she gazes at the tickets in her hand.*] I can't.

VIRGIL   But why?

PIM   Because that's not enough, Virgil. It all sounds lovely, of course, and I'm sure it really would be. . . . but only once. After that, there has to be a tomorrow. There has to be more. I need more, and there is no more for you.

VIRGIL   [*contrite*] I have made a fool of myself.

PIM   So have I.

VIRGIL   But you at least have the ability to make a different decision. You can change. I am bound to a script in which I had no say.

PIM   [*looks at the tickets in her hand*] I have to go. Thank you, Virgil.

VIRGIL   No, sweet lady, thank you. For all you have done. If it were not for the screen, I would kiss your lovely hand.

PIM   I appreciate the sentiment.

VIRGIL You shouldn't; it's dreadfully unoriginal.

PIM Goodbye, then. I'll see you soon.

VIRGIL Goodbye, my dear.

[*Pim EXITS. Virgil sighs. Shortly, Agnes RE-ENTERS, hanging her head.*]

AGNES [*despondent*] There's nothing in those books.

[*Virgil nods, sadly. Agnes reaches for him. He embraces her tightly. When they speak, their voices are sadder, resigned.*]

VIRGIL Speak in earnest now, Agnes; can you promise me your whole self? Tell me the truth, darling. I won't settle for anything less.

AGNES [*softly*] But Virgil, that is nothing I have to promise. . . . that is truth itself. Dearest, I am no self at all without you.

As they gaze into each other's eyes with this sad understanding, THE LIGHTS. . . .

FADE TO BLACK

END OF PLAY

Foul

BY LADARIAN SMITH

Copyright © by LaDarian Smith. All rights reserved. Published with permission from the author. Inquiries concerning rights should be addressed to LaDarian Smith at ladarian2014@gmail.com.

Foul

Presented October 25, 2013 | Kenan Theatre, UNC Department of Dramatic Art | Directed by Dana Coen

CHARACTERS

Original cast members are in brackets.

TYLER GREEN 19, male, African American basketball player [Kashif Powell].

DEBRA GREEN 48, female, African American, Tyler's mother [Kathy Atwater].

ERIC GREEN 48, male, African American, Tyler's father [Trevor Johnson].

TIME & SETTING

Present. An indoor basketball court.

LIGHTS UP

On an indoor basketball court. At the top of the stage a GAME CLOCK IS TICKING DOWN FROM 00:13.

TYLER GREEN, a tall black male wearing a basketball jersey and shorts, STORMS into the light, carrying a basketball. He's frantic and wide-eyed.

TYLER [breathless] Time! I SAID TIME!!!

[*The clock STOPS at 00:11.*]

TYLER [*to the audience*] Eleven seconds left in the fourth quarter. Score is seventy-nine to seventy-eight. I'm at half-court, ball in my hand, and sweat flying everywhere.

[*He takes a long beat and calms as he reflects on the moment.*]

TYLER I've been playing ball since I could walk. . . . rec leagues, summer camps, high school, all of it. Nothing ever came more naturally. It was my escape from everything and everyone. [*beat*] Except Drew. He made everything different.

[*DEBRA GREEN APPEARS. Tyler BOUNCES HER THE BALL.*]

DEBRA [*fuming*] What is wrong with you, Tyler? Out of all the things you could've been doing.

TYLER [*to Debra*] Mama, calm down!

DEBRA Boy, look at me. This is serious. You're lucky your coach caught you and not some big-mouth.

TYLER Please, list. . . .

DEBRA Who were you with?

TYLER What?

DEBRA Don't act like you can't hear me.

[*He turns away.*]

DEBRA [*her worst fear*] I knew it. Boy, are you crazy? I see Drew's mother every day at prayer, and you're down at the school doing this?

TYLER Coach didn't see who I was. . . .

DEBRA I thought basketball meant I wouldn't have to worry about things like this!

[*ERIC GREEN, Tyler's father, APPEARS from the other side.*]

[*Debra BOUNCES HIM THE BALL.*]

ERIC [*voice shaking*] All I could do is laugh at first. I say, "Tyler did what? You got to be mistaken." And then when it's quiet on the other end, it hits me like a damn train!

DEBRA Calm down before you hurt somebody. This is your son!

ERIC [*struggling to form the words*] My son. . . . is *not* a faggot.

DEBRA *Our* son. . . .

ERIC Don't act like I'm the only one that ain't happy right now! Too busy locked up in the church all day to notice. [*beat*] All that praying and speaking in tongues, and what do you get for it?

TYLER [*to Eric*] Yeah? And when's the last time you even set foot in a church? Or is the receptionist down at your shop the only person you have time for nowadays?

ERIC What I do down at my shop is none of your business. The money I make is what put those damn shoes on your feet and what sent you to those expensive camps. Those girls down at the school. . . . they don't catch your eye? You'd rather be sweet on another nigga' than a woman? Because I'm just trying to understand how this happens to a basketball player!

DEBRA Eric. . . .

[*Eric holds a hand out to silence her.*]

ERIC None of that even matters now. If this gets out, who do you think is going to put you on their team? Then what are you going to do?

[*Tyler has no answer for them. Eric BOUNCES THE BALL BACK TO TYLER. He and Debra EXIT on their respective sides of the stage.*]

TYLER [*to the audience*] He moved into my neighborhood. I remember meeting him on the court and watching him drive the ball to the net. He smiled the entire time, and I could tell he was in love with the game. I was the first person he picked to be on his team. Boys ever since. [*beat*] We got older and we'd compare sizes, and then laugh it off and throw some random girl in the conversation to make ourselves feel better. All of this right after morning workouts and before homeroom. [*beat*] But the looking turned into slight touches here and there. Then the touches became a grab. [*becoming rougher with the ball*] Then the grabs became rubs, and finally. . . .

[*Tyler SLAMS the ball down. It BOUNCES HIGH, then descends back into his arms.*]

TYLER [*to the audience*] I fought it. Went and slept with some of the baddest girls in school, waiting for my body to finally get the message. [*beat*] It never did. Nobody makes me angrier, more self-aware, more confused, and more vulnerable than Drew Anderson. I'm not saying we're "dumb athletes," but neither of us was getting any money to go to college for our grades. This was literally our only way out and if I wanted to keep it, for both me and for Drew, the best thing to do was to just let it go. Stealing glances and pretending to accidentally brush hands was the best we could do. [*beat*] He wanted to go to the same school, but I didn't. It was too much. I ended up in Kansas. He went to Syracuse. I'd hoped by getting away from everything it would give me a chance to think about what it was I wanted. But, it just made me angry at myself for pushing him away. Eventually, we stopped talking altogether.

[*Tyler STARTS DRIBBLING but handles the ball SLOPPILY.*]

TYLER [*to the audience*] My game was off. And practices weren't good because I felt like I couldn't see anyone. And I'm a point guard, so if I'm off then everyone feels it. My teammates ended up sitting me down just to make sure I was all right. [*beat*] Things wouldn't get better for some time, but once I'd made an effort to stop beating myself up, my game improved. We ended up making it to the final round of the NCAA tournament. I remember sitting in front of the TV, watching Syracuse play for the last spot and praying that they'd lose so I wouldn't have to play against Drew. [*beat*] But they didn't lose. And a week later I was face to face with him on the court. Everything about it felt right, even if his cold eyes said otherwise.

[*The GAME CLOCK RESTARTS. Tyler SIMULATES A GAME, running up and down the court, moving and juking.*]

TYLER   [*to the audience, picking up the moment from the top of the play*] Eleven seconds left. Not much time to do anything, but I have to try. No sooner than I'm passed the ball, I'm off! I feel Drew's angry breaths behind me as he tries to take the ball from my possession. I fake him out and storm past, watching him slide neatly across the floor and out of bounds. My heart is pounding through my ribs. I get a clear shot, take it. . . .

[*He SHOOTS. The ball CLANGS OFF THE RIM and bounces back to Tyler. The BUZZER sounds! The GAME CLOCK reads 0:00.*]

TYLER   [*to the audience, beat*] The arena is chaos. My eyes are racing to keep up with my thoughts. [*beat*] And then, there he is. The smile is back. . . . and just like that we are locked.

[*Tyler symbolically embraces his basketball, taking in the smell and feel of it.*]

TYLER   [*to the audience*] My ears are hot and I can feel tears burning my eyes. My head leans into the curve of his neck. I can hear the cameras clicking.

[*Debra and Eric APPEAR upstage from their opposite corners and stare down at Tyler. They are emotionless.*]

TYLER   [*to the audience*] I look up into the crowd to find my parents. I half expect them to come down from the stands and rip me from Drew's arms. [*beat*] So what do I do when none of this is supposed to happen? What do I say when words don't do anything? [*beat*] I listen.

[*Tyler DRIBBLES THE BALL rhythmically.*]

TYLER [*to the audience*] I hear his heart beating. Fast. Strong. Proud. I feel sedated by his pulse. I couldn't leave even if I thought about it. The sweat from his body swirls with mine and the breath on my neck is numbing. This is us, in high definition, embracing life itself and only stopping because the moment is up and we have to clear the court. I don't know what's going to happen next.

[*He STOPS DRIBBLING.*]

TYLER But I don't care.

BLACKOUT

END OF PLAY

Inside Out

BY LAURA STOLTZ

Copyright © by Laura Stoltz. All rights reserved. Published with permission from the author. Inquiries concerning rights should be addressed to Laura Stoltz at lestoltz@gmail.com.

Inside Out

Premiered October 6, 2011 | Swain Hall, Studio 6 Theatre, UNC Department of Communication | Directed by Dana Coen

CHARACTERS

Original cast members are in brackets.

ABIGAIL BENNETT 29, female, pregnant [Marie Garlock].

SEAN BENNETT 30, male, Abigail's husband [Jon Pipas].

TIME & SETTING

Present. The Bennett bedroom, specifically their bed.

SCENE ONE

LIGHTS UP

On the Bennett bedroom. ABIGAIL BENNETT, slight, is curled up on their queen-sized bed in a fetal position next to SEAN BENNETT.

ABIGAIL Margaret.

SEAN Hmm?

ABIGAIL Her name. Margaret.

[*Sean thinks it over for a moment.*]

SEAN [*trying to sound serious*] I was leaning more towards Shauna.

ABIGAIL [*kidding*] Oh, right. Sean and Shauna. Sounds great.

SEAN I see, you don't think I have good taste.

[*Sean TICKLES Abigail aggressively. She LAUGHS joyfully.*]

END OF SCENE

SCENE TWO

Sean and Abigail ENTER the bedroom. He is smiling. She wears loose clothing and carries a stuffed dog.

ABIGAIL I just. . . . thought you'd really want a boy, you know?

[*Abigail SITS on the edge of the bed. Sean joins her.*]

SEAN It doesn't matter what it is, as long as it's healthy.

[*This last word stings Abigail. Her mood changes slightly. Sean notices.*]

SEAN Everything's going to be fine, Abigail. There's going to be a miniature me running around. Picking her nose, scraping her knees. . . .

ABIGAIL I'm almost positive they do more than that. They cry and poop a lot, too.

SEAN [*off her concern*] What would make you happy right now?

ABIGAIL [*beat*] Pizza.

END OF SCENE

SCENE THREE

Sean and Abigail are in bed. Abigail is holding the stuffed dog in front of her stomach.

ABIGAIL Thanks for dinner.

SEAN Two dinners, you mean? You stole my breadsticks before I could even smell them.

[*Abigail shrugs sheepishly.*]

SEAN You looked like you were really enjoying it, though. [*patting the stuffed dog*] You'll be getting bigger before we know it!

[*Abigail's smile dims. The light goes out of her eyes. She places the stuffed dog between them.*]

END OF SCENE

SCENE FOUR

Sean is lying down on the bed. He yawns. Abigail ENTERS and quickly checks her face in the mirror, touching up the area around her mouth, making sure there's nothing in her hair, etc. She then crosses to the bed.

SEAN You okay?

ABIGAIL Yeah.

SEAN Why's your hair wet?

ABIGAIL Just washed my face.

[*She lies down on the bed, remains on her back, the stuffed dog between them.*]

SEAN [*yawning*] Okay.

[*Sean turns over on his side, facing away from Abigail. He closes his eyes.*]

ABIGAIL Well, good night.

SEAN [*sleepily*] Night, babe.

[*Abigail stares up at the ceiling.*]

END OF SCENE

SCENE FIVE

Late morning. Abigail lies on the bed watching television. Sean ENTERS.

ABIGAIL What'd you get?

SEAN Broccoli, cucumbers, chicken, beans, asparagus. . . .

ABIGAIL Enough green stuff?

SEAN Well, I hope the chicken isn't green.

ABIGAIL Anything that's not on the list?

[*From behind his back, Sean pulls out a small bag of cookies. He holds them up so she can see them. Abigail looks appalled.*]

SEAN Don't make me look like the bad guy. You can have them, but only after I get something healthy in you first.

[*Abigail reaches for the cookies. Sean evades her.*]

SEAN Just think about how much harder it'd be to lose all that baby weight if you only eat junk. You can deal with eating healthy for five months.

ABIGAIL [*seriously*] No, I can't. The thing is. . . .

SEAN [*cutting her off*] I don't exactly know what trans fats are, but they don't sound good and there are a lot of them in there.

ABIGAIL Didn't you hear me?

[*Sean hands the bag of cookies to Abigail.*]

SEAN Call you when dinner's ready.

[*Sean EXITS. An eager Abigail desperately struggles to open the bag.*]

END OF SCENE

SCENE SIX

Sean and Abigail are on their bed, playing video games. The stuffed dog remains between them. Abigail is winning. This is the norm.

ABIGAIL Can we order Chinese?

SEAN [*distracted*] I've got chicken in the oven.

ABIGAIL [*hopefully*] For. . . . chicken Parmesan?

SEAN Just chicken.

ABIGAIL We can save it for tomorrow.

[*Sean is focused on the game.*]

ABIGAIL I'd really, really like some lo mein. It's just one day.

[*No response from Sean.*]

ABIGAIL [*directly at him*] Or, you know, maybe we could just devour a small Somalian child.

[*Sean is winning now.*]

ABIGAIL [*serious*] I just think it'd make me feel better.

[*Sean celebrates his victory. Abigail RISES. She starts to exit.*]

SEAN Where're you going?

ABIGAIL I'll be back.

[*Abigail EXITS.*]

END OF SCENE

SCENE SEVEN

Later. Sean is sitting in the same spot on the bed. Abigail enters.

SEAN Leftovers are in the fridge.

ABIGAIL Sorry.

SEAN Where'd you go?

ABIGAIL I just needed to get out, clear my head.

SEAN Why?

ABIGAIL The doctor said it helps with stress.

[*Sean pats the place next to him on the sheet. Abigail sits next to him but doesn't get too close.*]

ABIGAIL Sean, we need to....

SEAN [*cutting her off*] I don't know how hormonal imbalance feels, but I'm guessing it sucks.

ABIGAIL No, I'm....

SEAN [*again cutting her off*] I know what we can do to make you feel better.

[*Abigail is hopeful.*]

SEAN I'll warm up the leftovers. You get grouchy on an empty stomach.

[*Sean rises. Abigail reaches for him, but he's already out of reach.*]

ABIGAIL No, really, I don't want any.

SEAN Oh, come on! You always want food.

[*Sean EXITS. Abigail looks sickened at the thought.*]

END OF SCENE

SCENE EIGHT

Abigail and Sean are SLEEPING. Abigail awakens, stirs, and looks at Sean. Seeing that he's still asleep, she quietly RISES AND EXITS.

END OF SCENE

SCENE NINE

Morning. Sean is at the mirror, getting ready. Abigail ENTERS. She looks pale.

SEAN [*suspicious*] Where were you? I woke up and you were gone.

ABIGAIL I went to pick up some baby stuff.

[*She tidies up around the room.*]

SEAN It's, like, eight o'clock in the morning.

[*Abigail doesn't respond.*]

SEAN So, where's the stuff?

ABIGAIL In the car.

SEAN [*suspicious*] What'd you get?

ABIGAIL I don't know, this and that.

SEAN Like what?

ABIGAIL [*aggravated*] Just stuff, okay?

SEAN I'm curious.

ABIGAIL [*beat*] Diapers.

SEAN [*skeptical*] Okay.

ABIGAIL I actually don't think I got enough. I may go back out later for more.

SEAN Were you out all night?

ABIGAIL No, of course not. Didn't you feel me get out of bed? I left about six.

[*Abigail lies down on the bed.*]

SEAN Maybe I'm just not used to you being gone in the morning or something. Puts crazy thoughts in my head.

ABIGAIL   Do you want to come and lie down?

SEAN   [*beat, caustic*] No. I think I'll go get some diapers.

[*Sean EXITS.*]

END OF SCENE

SCENE TEN

Abigail ENTERS, wiping her mouth with the back of her hand. Sean FOLLOWS.

SEAN   Why didn't you tell me you weren't feeling well?

ABIGAIL   It's not that. I. . . .

SEAN   [*cutting her off*] When did you start feeling bad?

ABIGAIL   I'm not. . . .

SEAN   [*cutting her off*] I knew I shouldn't have cooked that frozen chicken. I meant to throw it away, and then I was second-guessing myself and decided to use it anyway, and. . . .

ABIGAIL   [*exasperated*] For God's sake, I'm not sick! [*gaining in intensity*] I've put on ten pounds already, which I'm sure you've noticed, and I'm only halfway through, which means at least ten more, and there's nothing I can do about it! I've lost control over everything. You're going to have a fat wife, and everyone's going to talk about your fat wife, and you're going to start to believe them, and want a thin wife. I'm trying to be that thin wife, but I can't with this thing inside me! No, well, don't take that the wrong way. What I mean is, I love her, but she needs to come out. I don't know how much longer I can take it. How could you not notice? Honestly? I had vomit in my hair half the time! In my hair, Sean. I smelled like it, and I had it in my hair. Do you just not even want to look at me anymore? I can't blame you for that one. Who would want to? I know you've been looking for an excuse to leave, so just go. Just like my fucking father. Shut down, refuse to face the problem, act like nothing's wrong, act like. . . .

[*Abigail, winded and frustrated, pauses. Sean hands her the stuffed dog. She pulls it close to herself, cradling it.*]

SEAN Keep going. [*beat, serious*] I'm listening.

As he waits for her to continue, THE LIGHTS. . . .

FADE TO BLACK

END OF PLAY

Jumpers and Anchors

BY LAUREN WINN

Copyright © by Lauren Winn. All rights reserved. Published with permission from the author. Inquiries concerning rights should be addressed to Lauren Winn at laurennakaowinn@gmail.com.

Jumpers and Anchors

Presented October 25, 2013 | Kenan Theatre, UNC Department of Dramatic Art | Directed by Mark Cornell

CHARACTERS

Original cast members are in brackets.

NICK   19, male, troubled [Max Cullen].

DOUG   46, male, high-spirited [Trevor Johnson].

TIME & SETTING

Present. The railing of a large city's spanned bridge.

LIGHTS UP

On NICK. He's STANDING at the railing of a large bridge. A SOUNDSCAPE of various CITY-CENTRIC NOISES can be heard. . . . honking horns, cars driving, buses stopping. Nick is dressed in a black suit, but there's something disheveled about him. His tie is loose and uneven, a corner of his shirt is untucked, the fabric seems stretched and wrinkled at the same time. His hair is matted, and his face is red in some places and pallid in others. Nick GAZES below, eyes unfocused and burdened with angst, confusion, guilt, and lost purpose. He rests his hands on the top of the railing and looks directly down. He fidgets.

DOUG   [*offstage*] Would it be easier if I gave you a quarter?

[*DOUG APPEARS from behind a girder, which is off to one side. He is dressed in weekend get-up: a faded baseball cap, worn jeans, and an old plaid shirt. He has a bulky pack on his back. A digital SLR camera hangs from his neck.*]

NICK [*confused*] What?

DOUG A quarter.... to decide.

NICK [*incredulous*] It's not that simple.

DOUG Why not? You flip the coin and it tells you what to do. One minute you're here, the next you're gone. Sounds simple to me.

NICK I don't need your quarter. I already know where this ends.

DOUG [*inching forward*] Do you?

NICK Stay back!

DOUG I'm not going to do anything.

[*Nick climbs onto the railing.*]

NICK Any closer and I jump.

DOUG I didn't come up here to see some kid kill himself. Let's talk.

NICK There's nothing to talk about.

DOUG I think there's plenty.

NICK Leave me alone.

DOUG You got a name?

NICK Why do you care?

DOUG Just want to know your name.

NICK It's Nick.

DOUG Nick then. Nick, have you ever wondered what it would be like to live forever?

NICK What does it matter; it's impossible.

DOUG Is it? How does man become immortal?

NICK What kind of question is that?

[*Doug lifts his camera and takes a photo of Nick. He checks the image on the LCD screen on the back, nods in approval.*]

DOUG You're photogenic, Nick. But it'd be better if you smiled.

[*Doug fiddles with a setting on his camera before pointing it again at Nick. Nick twitches uncomfortably as he stares at the water below.*]

NICK I have no reason to.

DOUG [*lowering the camera*] Sure you do.

NICK Why, because an old guy like you thinks he can talk me out of jumping?

[*Doug lifts the camera again. He pans Nick's face with it, his left eye squinting in concentration.*]

DOUG I'm not that old. And I never said I was going to talk you out of it.

[*He takes a photo.*]

DOUG But, look here.

[*Doug closes the distance between them.*]

NICK Hey!

DOUG Easy. I just want you to see this photo.

[*Doug extends the camera's LCD screen toward Nick.*]

DOUG See this? This is proof of your existence. If you jump, right now, you leave this behind. Whatever happens to you, this photo stays.

NICK That doesn't make me immortal.

DOUG No, but your actions do. Think. If you jump here, you'll be remembered as a jumper. If you don't jump, do something with your life that affects someone else, that's what will be remembered. You could be someone's anchor. [*long beat*] How old do you think this camera is?

NICK [*studying the bulky digital SLR*] I don't know. It looks new.

DOUG Yeah, it does. It's eight years old. I got it for my birthday. Always wanted to use it but never had the time. . . . too focused with work. It's just one of many things I've wanted to do.

NICK So do them.

DOUG I am. [*beat*] Do you have anything you wish you could do?

NICK [*beat*] Maybe say goodbye.

DOUG What's stopping you? You don't even have to say goodbye. Go back and appreciate those you would leave behind.

NICK You don't get it! He's gone already! I'm alone. I have no one! He was all I had left! I have nobody. You understand? No one.

DOUG Trust me, I do. Truth is, and I'm not lying. . . . I came here to jump too. I want to know if you're going to do it because I don't want to go alone.

NICK [*stunned*] You can't be serious.

DOUG I am.

NICK Whatever happened to all that jumpers and anchors crap? Get the hell away from me.

[*Doug CHUCKLES in response.*]

NICK And why are you laughing!?

[*Doug removes his backpack and hunches down to retrieve its contents. He holds up a BUNGEE CORD AND HARNESS. Doug steps into the harness before pulling and snapping it tight. Nick looks on with astonishment.*]

DOUG Now look where we are.

[*Doug pulls out ANOTHER BUNGEE HARNESS.*]

DOUG Always carry two in case one fails. [*beat*] So Nick, what'll it be?

[*Nick stares back incredulously. Doug waits patiently. Shortly, Nick looks down from the bridge.*]

NICK How would we get back up?

DOUG Cops will help us. Saw a guy over there make a call. They're probably on their way.

NICK What!?

DOUG The cops. They're on their way up here to stop us from jumping. Which is exactly why we should do it now! Let's give them something to talk about at the station.

[*A ghost of a smile flashes across Nick's face. He's filled with nervous excitement.*]

DOUG Whaddya say?!

[*POLICE SIRENS echo from offstage.*]

NICK [*softly*] Okay.

[*Nick pulls on his harness and snaps it into place. Doug checks to ensure that it's attached properly. They snap on the carabiners of the bungee cords before locking them in. They CLIMB ONTO THE SIDE OF THE BRIDGE. Nick looks intimidated.*]

DOUG Having doubts?

NICK I don't suppose you have a quarter on you?

DOUG [*laughing*] I don't.

[*Nick braces himself and steps closer to the side. Doug lifts his camera and pulls Nick into the frame view.*]

DOUG Smile.

[*They both smile. Doug takes a selfie of them, then secures the camera onto his harness with a carabiner.*]

DOUG Okay, on one. . . .

NICK . . . . two. . . .

BLACKOUT

DOUG and NICK Three!

END OF PLAY

Acknowledgments

I would like to thank the following for their contributions to the development of the Long Story Shorts One Act Festival:

Dominic Abbenante	Paul Ferguson	Michael Rolleri
Laura Azar	Andrea Ferguson	Tim Scales
McKay Coble	Rob Hamilton	Jennifer Stander
Wesley Darling	Natasha Jackson	Sharon Van Vechten
Ray Dickie	Dane Keil	Jacob Wishnek
Thomas Gamble	Joseph Megel	
Bonnie Gould	David Navalinsky	

And a very special thanks to **Rosemarie Kitchin,** who has served as the festival's associate producer since 2014 and worked tirelessly on the formatting and copy editing of this volume.

Editor's Biography

DANA COEN is the director of the UNC Writing for the Screen and Stage program, a two-year interdisciplinary minor, in which selected students study the craft of dramatic writing in preparation for careers in theatre, film, and television. He is the creator, artistic director, and producer of Long Story Shorts and Activated Art, an ekphrastic theatre festival presented in collaboration with the Ackland Art Museum.

A former New York actor and director, Dana has written extensively for both television and the theatre. He was co-executive producer and writer on the Fox prime-time series *Bones*, and co-executive producer on the CBS prime-time series *JAG*, where he spent eight seasons and wrote thirty-seven episodes. Other credits include a comedy development deal for Walt Disney Studios; story editor on the comedy *Room for Two*, starring Linda Lavin and Patricia Heaton; and staff writer on *Carol and Company*, starring Carol Burnett. He has also written pilot scripts for ABC, NBC, Fox, Paramount Television, and MCA/Universal Television. Screenwriting awards include the 2003 Jewish Image Award and the 1999 Templeton Prize.

As a playwright, Dana's produced work includes *Property* at the Carrboro Arts Center's Redbird Play Festival, Los Angeles productions of *Internal Bleeding* at the Pacific Repertory Theatre, *Tinkle Time* at Showtime's Act One Festival, *Bunches of Betty* at the West End Playhouse, and *Sympathy*, which was produced at both the Burbank Theatre Guild and Off Broadway at the Manhattan Punchline Theatre.

www.ingramcontent.com/pod-product-compliance
Lightning Source LLC
Chambersburg PA
CBHW031136160426
43193CB00008B/161